Flannery O'Connor

D1287605

FLANNERY O'CONNOR

Preston M. Browning, Jr.

WIPF & STOCK · Eugene, Oregon

Wipf and Stock Publishers
199 W 8th Ave, Suite 3
Eugene, OR 97401

Flannery O'Connor
The Coincidence of the Holy and the Demonic in O'Connor's Fiction
By Browning, Preston M., Jr.
Copyright©1974 Browning, Preston M., Jr.
ISBN 13: 978-1-60608-534-9
Publication date 8/13/2009
Previously published by Southern Illinois University Press, 1974

A number of people have aided, directly or indirectly, in the writing of this book, and I am happy to have this opportunity to express my gratitude. First to my father, Preston M. Browning, Sr., who over the years has given assistance of various kinds and whose generosity it is impossible to acknowledge adequately. Then to Nathan Scott, who first suggested that I undertake a study of Flannery O'Connor's fiction and who guided the work through its earliest development. Jim Miller offered encouragement, as did, later on, Jim Stronks, Nancy Cirillo and Edith Hartnett, whose reading of a preliminary draft made for considerable stylistic improvement. Dorothy McFarland read the entire manuscript and responded with criticism as probing as it was judicious. To Giles Gunn and Ben McKulik I owe a long-standing debt of gratitude. The former's knowledge and love of American literature continues to serve as both a model and a challenge, while the latter's unflagging enthusiasm for Flannery O'Connor and his dedication to the creative teaching of her and other modern authors have influenced me in more ways than he probably knows. To the students in my seminar on "Images of Absurdity in Contemporary American Fiction" and particularly to Tom O'Brien, whose unpublished paper on *Wise Blood* furnished a number of the ideas for my chapter on that novel, I wish to express my appreciation. I have, in several instances, retained the language of that essay. Minerva Bell typed the manuscript with patience and care.

Finally, there is Ann, to whom, at this juncture, thanks seem a trifle ridiculous but without whom the book would not be and for whom the book is.

PRESTON M. BROWNING, JR.

University of Illinois at Chicago Circle
January 17, 1974

Series Foreword

Forty-five years after her death, Flannery O'Connor continues to interest readers. Graduate students write theses and scholars publish books analyzing her work. During this spring of 2009, a major biography of O'Connor was published and reviewed nationally. O'Connor's readership is not limited to academicians. According to on-line book dealers, her books continue to sell well.

O'Connor first received critical attention in the popular press, which reviewed her first novel, *Wise Blood*. Early reviewers were unsure of what to make of the religious struggles of Hazel Motes, O'Connor's "saint in spite of himself." Many reviewers tried to place O'Connor in a convenient pigeonhole labeled "Southern Gothic," suggesting that her work was a pale imitation of William Faulkner, Carson McCullers, Truman Capote and, less favorably, Erskine Caldwell. One reviewer, objecting to the violence of some of her stories, called her work "highly unladylike." O'Connor's early reviewers often failed to see the depths in her work.

The late 1950s brought the beginning of serious academic inquiry into O'Connor's fiction. In 1958, *Critique* devoted an entire issue to articles on O'Connor and another Catholic author, J. F. Powers. In 1962, *The Sewanee Review* published her novella, "The Lame Shall Enter First," and John Hawkes' important article, "Flannery O'Connor's Devil."

Books on O'Connor began to appear in the mid-1960s, after her death. Stanley Edgar Hyman wrote a short monograph on her work as part of the "Pamphlets on American Writers" series published by the University of Minnesota Press. Vanderbilt University Press published Carter W. Martin's study *The True Country: Themes in the Fiction of Flannery O'Connor* in 1968. These volumes were useful introductions to major themes in her work, but more books were to follow.

The early 1970s saw the publication of valuable books on O'Connor. Preston M. Browning published one of the best general introductions to O'Connor's life and work. Martha Stephens' *The Question of Flannery O'Connor* examined O'Connor's seemingly harsh, austere Christian worldview. Scholars like John R. May and David Eggenschwiler paid particular attention to the religious underpinnings of her fiction. May examined her stories as modern-day parables. Eggenschwiler related her work and thought to modern theology. Josephine Hendin took the controversial step of looking at autobiographical elements in the stories. In her book, Carol Shloss suggested that O'Connor addressed her work to "those [readers] who are untutored in religious belief" in an effort to make it accessible to readers of any religious persuasion.

These books were originally published in small print runs by university presses and have long since gone out of print. Wipf & Stock's Flannery O'Connor Studies Series brings some of these important books back into print for contemporary readers. They will help readers gain greater insight into O'Connor's art. All the authors are living, though some have retired from teaching. Their work on O'Connor came early in their careers. Each scholar has continued to work in academia and to publish books on other literary subjects. They have graciously granted Wipf &

Series Foreword

Stock permission to bring their early books back into circulation. The casual reader and the academic will learn much about the life and art of Flannery O'Connor from these studies.

Douglas Robillard, Jr.
Series Editor for the Flannery O'Connor Studies Series
University of Arkansas at Pine Bluff
March 2009

Contents

Preface to the 2009 Edition

By the time my study of Flannery O'Connor's fiction was published by Southern Illinois University Press in 1974, it was beginning to become clear that an "O'Connor industry" was under way. O'Connor had been dead for just under a decade and already there were seven or eight books devoted to her work. Today there are more than ninety, with titles suggesting an enormous range of topics. Here are two, picked more or less at random: *Flannery O'Connor: Literary Prophet of the South* and *Flannery O'Connor and Cold War Culture*. There are, in addition, hundreds of articles about her works in literary journals published in North America as well as France and other countries.

My study of O'Connor focused largely on the religious dimensions of her fiction, as did most of the other studies published at that time. As the seventies and eighties rolled along, however, academic writers began to closely examine aspects of the fiction which had been neglected by earlier O'Connor scholars, most notably O'Connor's treatment of blacks and women. Her attitude toward sex, too, came in for rather heated debate, for the fiction itself suggests that this author found it difficult to treat this central aspect of human life at all realistically.

That O'Connor was, in fact, made extremely uncomfortable by the reality of sex as a constitutive feature of human relations became clear with the publication, in 1979, of the sizeable collection of her letters, *The Habit of Being,* edited by Sally Fitzgerald. In some of her correspondence she confesses that she did not want to grow past the age of twelve and that the courtship rituals of adolescence were repugnant to her. This volume, of course, was invaluable in giving all of us who had read and reread her stories and novels a deeper appreciation of the complexity of the mind and heart of this superbly gifted writer.

Subsequently, biographical studies have appeared but none to match the recently-published *Flannery: A Life of Flannery O'Connor* by Brad Gooch. Gooch was meticulous in tracking down relatives, classmates, literary correspondents, agents and publishers whose remembrances have added immeasurably to our appreciation of the journey that took this rather awkward five-year-old child in Savanna, Georgia, with a chicken that walked backwards, to literary fame and the posthumous honoring of her *Complete Stories* in 1972 with the National Book Award in Fiction.

On the occasion of the award ceremony, O'Connor's friend and publisher, Robert Giroux, spoke words which sum up more poignantly than any I might write the qualities which have drawn loyal readers to Flannery O'Connor and her stories for decades: "In an age of mendacity, duplicity and document-shredders, the clear vision of Flannery O'Connor not only burns brighter than ever but it burns through the masks of what she called 'blind wills and low dodges of the heart.'"

I have no doubt that Flannery O'Connor will find avid readers and admirers for many years to come.

Preston Browning
March 2009

1

The Background: Life, Works, and Reputation

One of Flannery O'Connor's characters, a woman of aristocratic Southern ancestry, remarks: "If you know who you are, you can go anywhere." Flannery O'Connor knew, I suspect, who she was and she went a long way with that knowledge. So far, in fact, that she became an enigma to plain readers and critics alike, an enigma which tantalizes and teases and sometimes frustrates. Her life, on the surface seeming relatively simple, appears on close examination not simple at all. Like her fiction, it has depths which beckon, which promise revelation, but which finally lead the gazer to a pinpoint of light. And there he waits, staring at the pinpoint, hoping for further illumination. It may come. But the pinpoint of light remains elusive and leads, invariably, to greater depths. That is to say, to mystery, which is what Flannery O'Connor, as well as her fiction, is all about.

Born on March 25, 1925, she was baptized Mary Flannery O'Connor. Twenty some years later, ready to embark on a career as a writer of fiction, she dropped the first name, having decided that Mary O'Connor on the dust jacket would do little to enhance the appeal of a book. Both her parents came from old Georgia families and both were Roman Catholic. The O'Connors were from Savannah, where Flannery was born. Her mother's family, the Clines, had long been established in Milledgeville, Regina Cline's father for many years serving it as mayor.[1]

Mary Flannery was an only child and one who at an early age displayed an interest in the unusual, the off-beat, the abnormal—a penchant which would one day become the hallmark of her fiction. In an essay on raising peafowl, written for *Holiday* in 1961, Miss O'Connor records her early interest in the eccentric, telling of how she was filmed at age five with a pet bantam hen able to walk backwards and forward. In the same essay she notes that she "favored those with one green eye and one orange. . . . I wanted one with three legs or three wings but nothing in that line turned up."[2] Something like them did turn up eventually, human varieties at any rate, inventions of her ever-fertile imagination.

In Savannah, Flannery attended parochial schools and no doubt would have completed a Catholic high school education had not the discovery in her father of lupus, an incurable disease which mainly affects the blood vessels, caused the family to remove to Milledgeville in 1938. There the O'Connors lived in an ante-bellum brick house, which had been in the Cline family since 1886, and where Mary Flannery was to live during her high school and college years. There Edward O'Connor died in 1941.

At Peabody High School Flannery received an indifferent literary education (or so her lecture on the teaching of literature clearly implies), but she had early evinced a talent for drawing, which she nurtured at school and later at the Georgia State College for Women in Milledgeville, from which she graduated in 1945. For the college paper she did cartoons, using linoleum wood cuts, and for the yearbook of 1945 humorous drawings. Robert Fitzgerald, for many years her close friend and now her literary executor, records that the artistic work of this period already exhibited "the authentic O'Connor humor" and that her paintings, done after her literary career was well under way, are "soundly composed and bold and sensitive in color and revelatory of their subjects" [3]—an apt description of her creations in language as well.

As editor of the college literary magazine, Flannery demonstrated sufficient promise to win a fellowship to the creative writing program at the University of Iowa. Two years in Iowa produced an M.A., a thesis containing six stories, some of which would later be published, and an already launched writing career ("The Geranium" appeared in *Accent* in the summer of 1946). From Iowa City Flannery went on to Yaddo, a writers' colony at Saratoga Springs, for a brief stay and thence to New York. There occurred two fortunate events which contributed significantly to her career: she met Robert and Sally Fitzgerald, who provided encouragement as well as introductions to other young writers and to some of the more established members of New York's literati. And she met Robert Giroux, who would later become her editor and subsequently her publisher. For a time the Fitzgeralds became Flannery's "adopted kin" (the phrase is hers) when, as their boarder, she accompanied them to a newly-purchased house in Connecticut in the summer of 1949. The arrangement was, apparently, a happy one for all parties, Flannery spending her days working on a manuscript which was to become *Wise Blood* and her evenings discussing literary or religious topics with the Fitzgeralds or telling them stories of life "down home."

This idyll in the Connecticut countryside ended abruptly in December of 1950 when, on the train to Atlanta, Flannery became seriously ill with an ailment later diagnosed as lupus, the disease which had killed her father. The disease was checked by medication but its effects were sufficiently debilitating that a return to the life of an independent writer in the North was out of the question. Instead, Mrs. O'Connor took Flannery to Andalusia, a dairy farm some miles from Milledgeville, where she spent the remaining fourteen years of her life. And productive years they were! *Wise Blood*, the result of years of work and three major revisions, came out in 1952. In addition to "The Geranium," six stories had already appeared in magazines of the reputation of *Mademoiselle* and *Partisan Review*. Of these, four were incorporated into *Wise Blood*, generally after extensive reworking. From 1952 onwards there came a steady outpouring of stories, many of which won awards and were reprinted in one or both of the annual collections *Best Short Stories* and *The O. Henry Awards*. By 1955 Flannery realized that she had ample material for a collection and in the spring of that year Harcourt, Brace brought out *A Good Man Is Hard to Find*. Not all of the reviews were laudatory, though an unmistakable impression had been made: here was a talent of unusual depth and power, one displaying an ear for language which was unerringly right and an eye for human frailties which was remarkably sensitive.

The rewards of those years were not all honorary. In 1953 Miss O'Connor received a Kenyon Review Fellowship. When it was renewed the following year, she wrote to Robert Fitzgerald in her usual wry manner that "the Rockerfellers [sic] . . . will see to my blood and ACTH [the drug she was then using] for another year and I will have to keep on praying for the repose of John D.'s soul." [4] In 1959 the Ford Foundation awarded her a grant. The next year *The Violent Bear It Away*, a draft portion of which had appeared in *New World Writing* in 1955, was published amid general acclaim. With a collection of stories and two novels in print, Flannery had become something which apparently she never grew accustomed to being: a celebrity. Interviewers began to show up at Andalusia and Miss O'Connor's work drew increasing attention in the literary journals. Moreover, invitations to lecture started to come in, and during the late fifties and early sixties she made more than twenty visits to colleges and universities, lecturing to students and faculty and participating in symposia on writing. Her trip to Chicago in February (probably the worst month for a Southerner on crutches to visit that city) of 1959 to lecture at the University of Chicago resulted in a friendship with Richard Stern, and that part of their correspondence which he has published is memorable for intimations of Flannery's unfailing cheerfulness, even in particularly trying circumstances.[5]

In the spring of 1958 she made a trip of an altogether different sort. At the invitation of her Cousin Katie in Savannah, Flannery and her mother accompanied a group from that city on a pilgrimage to Lourdes, where, according to Fitzgerald, she "dreaded a miracle." None occurred, but the continued productivity of her imagination during the ensuing six years was a miracle of its own kind, in view of limitations imposed by her illness. This period produced "The Enduring Chill," "The Lame Shall Enter First," and "Parker's Back," which would later take their places beside "Greenleaf," the winner of the first prize in the O. Henry contest of 1956, in the posthumous collection *Everything That Rises Must Converge* (1965).

During these years Miss O'Connor corresponded with a large number of fellow writers, including, in addition to Richard Stern, John Hawkes, Katherine Anne Porter, and Caroline Gordon. The latter had given invaluable advice for the final revision of *Wise Blood* and Flannery O'Connor held her opinions in particularly high regard. During these same years Miss O'Connor's reading was

considerable in extent and varied in scope. Sr. Kathleen
Feeley, who in her study *Flannery O'Connor: Voice of
the Peacock* [6] makes extensive use of annotated and
underlined passages in books in the O'Connor library,
indicates the range of this reading: works by such classi-
cal theologians as Augustine and Aquinas, numerous
studies of Old Testament history and theology, books on
the Christian imagination and Christian symbolism,
writings of mystics such as St. Theresa. Marginal annotations suggest that she read with appreciation Mircea
Eliade's *The Sacred and the Profane* and *Patterns in
Comparative Religion,* as well as Carl Jung's *Modern
Man in Search of a Soul.* Also included in her library
were works by John Henry Newman, Martin Buber,
Maritain and Heidegger. Henry James was well represented, and the annotations in Richard Chases's *The
American Novel and Its Tradition* suggest that Flannery
found her reading of it especially profitable. Then, of
course, there was Teilhard de Chardin. Her enthusiasm
for his writings was quite uninhibited, and the following
passage from her review of *The Phenomenon of Man*
underscores the affinity she felt between his vision of
creation and her own: "His is a scientific expression of
what the poet attempts to do: penetrate matter until
spirit is revealed in it. Teilhard's vision sweeps forward
without detaching itself at any point from the earth.
. . . The poet, whose sight is essentially prophetic, will
at once recognize in Teilhard a kindred spirit." [7] She
requested the editor of *The Bulletin,* the Georgia dioc-
esan weekly, to send her for review any of Teilhard's
books he might lay his hands on, and between 1960 and
1963 she reviewed a total of seven books by or about
him. Clearly she found in Teilhard's thought much that
was congenial to her own and, despite a fundamental
difference in their conceptions of the nature of evil, it
seems indisputable that a good deal of the inspiration
for the stories in *Everything That Rises Must Converge*

derives from the Jesuit paleontologist-philosopher, from whose *The Phenomenon of Man* she borrowed the line which became the volume's title. Her reading thus suggests that for all of her joking reference to "interleck-chuls" in her letters to friends in the North and despite the harsh treatment she accorded the would-be intellectuals in her fiction, Miss O'Connor's respect for the life of the mind was profound and her own intellectual attainments considerable.

This becomes evident as one reads the collection *Mystery and Manners,* a volume of occasional prose selected by Robert and Sally Fitzgerald and published in 1969. In none of these pieces does Flannery O'Connor pretend to possess the specialized knowledge and skill of the professional critic. Yet how frequently she goes to the heart of a thorny problem with insights which, if not always strikingly original, place the question in a perspective which allows even the uninitiated to grasp its significance. When discussing the problem of literature and belief, for example, an issue with which critics of the stature of Erich Heller and T. S. Eliot have wrestled, and not always successfully, she makes this telling observation:

> you don't write fiction with assumptions. The things we see, hear, smell, and touch affect us long before we believe anything at all, and the South impresses its image on us from the moment we are able to distinguish one sound from another. By the time we are able to use our imaginations for fiction, we find that our senses have responded irrevocably to a certain reality. . . . What the Southern Catholic writer is apt to find, when he descends within his imagination, is not Catholic life but the life of this region in which he is both native and alien. He discovers that the imagination is not free, but bound.[8]

In her judgment, living in the Protestant South was a distinct advantage, for, as it becomes "more and more difficult in America to make belief believable," the

Catholic writer who is a Southerner has ready to hand the material of a culture which, as she often observed, is still Christ-haunted if no longer Christ-centered. More especially it is the familiarity of the Bible to the common people of the South which provides the Catholic novelist with an ethos whose spiritual habits and interests are congruent with his own most urgent preoccupations. In a lecture entitled "The Catholic Novelist in the Protestant South," she noted in this regard that

> in the South the Bible is known by the ignorant . . . and it is always that *mythos* which the poor hold in common that is most valuable to the fiction writer. When the poor hold sacred history in common, they have ties to the universal and the holy, which allows the meaning of their every action to be heightened and seen under the aspect of eternity.[9]

In much of her fiction the interpenetration of the temporal and the eternal is the force which drives the action forward to consummation.

The convergence of Catholic dogma and fundamentalist Protestant belief was, however, a peculiar mating, and Miss O'Connor did not minimize the difficulties which this alliance entailed: "The Catholic novelist in the South," she remarked, "is forced to follow the spirit into strange places and to recognize it in many forms not totally congenial to him."[10] Yet she saw in the fanaticism and bizarre practices of Southern Protestantism a kinship with the religious fervor of biblical faith. Here was a form of Christianity still capable of begetting fearless prophets and dedicated evangelists, men and women in whom conviction burned as fiercely as it had in Amos and Jeremiah, Paul and Stephen. And when compared with the conformism, the aimless pleasure seeking, and the spiritual somnolence which in her view characterized the general tenor of American life, the unflinching commitment to Christ of fundamentalist Christianity seemed far to outweigh the excesses to which it was prone.

If Flannery O'Connor was keenly aware of her somewhat odd situation as a Roman Catholic in the South where she was thus "both native and alien," she was no less sensitively attuned to her anomalous position as a believer in an age when belief was frequently dismissed as superstition or psychological aberration. Yet she recognized behind the oftentimes bland superiority of such attitudes a profound spiritual disquietude, and, wishing to do justice to this phenomenon, spoke of our era as one which "at its best . . . is an age of searchers and discoverers." [11] This spirit of search was not foreign to her own work and its potency in such stories as "A Good Man Is Hard to Find," "Parker's Back" and *Wise Blood* is evidence that, however physically isolated she may have been while living at Andalusia, she was not isolated from the major intellectual and spiritual currents of her time. Commenting upon the types of men which an unbelieving age produces, she called attention to the "man who can neither believe nor contain himself in unbelief and who searches desperately, feeling about in all experience for the lost God." [12] Just how fully Flannery O'Connor herself comprehended and participated in the spiritual travail of an age which has witnessed the "eclipse of God" is disclosed in the following confession: "[t]hese unbelieving searchers have their effect upon those of us who do believe. We begin to examine our own religious notions, to sound them for genuineness, to purify them in the heat of our unbelieving neighbor's anguish. What Christian novelist could compare his concern to Camus'?" [13]

Flannery O'Connor's preoccupation with the spiritual condition of modern man thus led her to write fiction of a peculiar cast, but her religious concerns fortified rather than weakened the artistic integrity of her creations. Such, at any rate, would seem to be the testimony of literary scholarship in the decade following her death. Reviews of the posthumously published volume of stories, *Everything That Rises Must Converge* (1965), were overwhelmingly favorable, one reviewer declaring it "the best collection of shorter fiction to have been published in America during the past 20 years." [14] Assessments of her overall achievement were equally lavish in praise. In a lengthy review article of her final collection, Warren Coffey spoke of her entire literary production as "work of an imaginative order and brilliance rare in the world at most times, perhaps always in American writing." [15] And John Hawkes, himself a novelist of extraordinary talent, included Flannery O'Connor, along with Quevedo, Lautrémont, Céline, Nathanael West and Joseph Heller, in the tradition of the "true" *avant garde* which he so admires. [16] Eight years later it appears certain that Flannery O'Connor has gained a permanent place among the distinguished writers of fiction—or of the short story, at any rate—in America.

Since her death, the critical interest in her work has grown at an astonishing pace, combined with a lessening of the widespread misunderstanding with which her fiction was originally greeted. No longer are the grotesque aspects of her stories considered "gratuitous," nor is she any longer categorized by means of the stereotypes which reviewers once applied almost indiscriminately to novelists from below the Mason-Dixon Line. Occasionally she was cited as "another southern Gothic novelist," and her work was abused or dismissed for its presumed nonfunctional horror and violence. This initial misunderstanding of her fiction resulted in large part from the failure of reviewers, and many critics, to discern the significant features which mark the creative imagination of Flannery O'Connor as radically different from that of other Southern writers such as Carson McCullers and Truman Capote. But equally important is the fact that the surface of Flannery O'Connor's work affords little to distinguish it from the writing of her Southern contemporaries. Crime and violence arise as naturally from her literary talent as do her razor sharp wit and her marvelously acute sense of the banality and absurdity of popular sayings, song lyrics, and advertising slogans. Her fiction abounds in grotesque situations and many of her most memorable characters are driven, "possessed" individuals. Freaks, fanatics, and psychopaths stalk the unfriendly streets and desolate clay roads of her fictional world, which often appears designed to simulate as nearly as possible a chamber of horrors. Thus can one explain the confused and sometimes hostile reaction of those who, in the early and middle 1950s, saw in Flannery O'Connor a disciple of the nihilistic-deterministic writers spawned by the Depression and the Second World War and the spiritual and cultural stagnation which followed them.

Yet Flannery O'Connor's own estimate of her vocation could not be more seriously religious: "I don't think you should write something as long as a novel around anything that is not of the gravest concern to you and everybody else and for me this is always the conflict between an attraction for the Holy and the disbelief in it that we breathe in with the air of the times." [17] It is almost certainly this rare coincidence of apparently opposing forces and motifs in her life and work which has often made Flannery O'Connor a puzzling figure. Here, at the point where the opposites coincide, where violent crime and "attraction for the Holy" are held in tension, is the point of departure of the present study. For it is my conviction that out of this tension grew Flannery O'Connor's extraordinary creative power and unique vision.

A glance at her two novels and one of her stories may serve to establish the centrality of this yoking of opposites in Flannery O'Connor's work. The protagonists of both *Wise Blood* and *The Violent Bear It Away* are driven to fulfill a destiny given shape by "an attraction for the Holy," though each commits murder in the process and each would seem, by most standards of health and normality, to be a fearfully twisted human being. In one of her early short pieces, a pathological killer known as The Misfit murders an entire family while proclaiming that Jesus "thown [sic] everything off balance." Ideally, The Misfit argues, one should follow His teachings: but since there is no possibility of ascertaining that Jesus was what he claimed to be, one is left with the agony of doubt and had therefore best enjoy himself by " 'doing some . . . meanness,' " " 'killing somebody or burning down his house.' " Only in such nihilistic acts is pleasure to be found and even this gratification, The Misfit sadly confesses, is more illusory than real.

The crime and violence and the apparent nihilism of some of Miss O'Connor's characters combine with a recurring "Hound of Heaven" motif to suggest an imagination in many respects similar to that of Dostoevsky. Flannery O'Connor's statement concerning the Christian writer's predilection for the grotesque partially explains this strange juxtaposition of seemingly alien elements in her writings:

> My own feeling is that writers who see by the light of their Christian faith will have, in these times, the sharpest eyes for the grotesque, for the perverse, and for the unacceptable.

> . . . .
> The novelist with Christian concerns will find in modern life distortions which are repugnant to him, and his problem will be to make these appear as distortions to an

audience which is used to seeing them as natural; and he
may well be forced to take ever more violent means to
get his vision across to this hostile audience. . . . to the
hard of hearing you shout, and for the almost-blind you
draw large and startling figures.[18]

Miss O'Connor's own explanation of her affinity for
distortion and violence must be taken seriously, though
it is arguable that her artistic vision is more ambiguous
and complex than her statement suggests. In my assess-
ment, this vision is constructed of an extremely delicate
blending of what seems to be totally incompatible ways
of apprehending reality. On the one hand there is the
espoused, orthodox Christian understanding of man.
Alongside it one finds a traditional though qualified
Southern view of human nature manifest in her satiric
attacks upon the materialism, secularism, and liberal
optimism of contemporary life. On the other hand there
appears to be an attraction for the extreme, the perverse, the violent, and for the grotesque for its own sake
and not merely as a fictional technique, which calls to
mind Thomas Mann's comment (he was thinking of
Dostoevsky and Nietzsche) that "certain attainments of
the soul and the intellect are impossible without disease,
without insanity, without spiritual crime." [19] Spiritual
crime: here is a concept paradoxical enough to illu-
minate some of Flannery O'Connor's most puzzling
stories.

A summary of my thesis concerning this religious
vision should aid in orienting the reader, alerting him to
elements which will be developed later. Briefly, my con-
clusions are that Flannery O'Connor's work may be
conceived as an effort to recover the idea of the Holy in
an age in which both the meaning and the reality of this
concept have been obscured; that she perceived that loss
of the Holy involved for contemporary man a concomitant loss of "depth" and a subsequent diminution

of being; and that she further understood that in re-
claiming depth and being (filling the "ontological void"
posited by Ionesco and other modern writers), contemporary man might very well become involved in a
journey through the radically profane, embracing evil in
order to rediscover good, pursuing the demonic in order
finally to arrive at the Holy. The journey upon which
she set many of her most unforgettable characters entails, in short, "spiritual crime"—crime whose ultimate
motive is a desperate desire to affirm a basis for human
existence which transcends the waywardness and will-
fulness of the individual human self.

But the quest for being or the Holy is only one side
of Flannery O'Connor's creative enterprise. The other
is her portrayal of the world of unbelief within which
that quest occurs. When she spoke of "the disbelief in
[the Holy] which we breathe in with the air of the
times," "the times" clearly embraced for her a good
deal more than mid-twentieth-century America. Yet, in
a special sense, it was the ethos of the 1950s against
which Miss O'Connor's stories were directed. I use
"against" deliberately, for Miss O'Connor was a satirist
of extraordinary vigor, and, in a decade when "positive
thinking" was as much a part of the American way of
life as cookouts and rock-and-roll, Flannery O'Connor
produced a magnificent assortment of stories, many of
which might well have been entitled "The Power of
Negative Thinking."

Gifted with an imagination delicately attuned to the
nuances of manners and folkways, Flannery O'Connor
detected in the manners of the 1950s such smugness,
optimism, and self-righteousness that only the harshest
attack could hope to move them. She also perceived, at
the root of this shallow complacency, what she felt to be
a fatuous belief in the omnipotence of a highly rational-
ized, technological society whose manipulation of human

beings is calculated to turn out, as an end product, persons like a character in *Wise Blood* who is said to be "so well-adjusted that she didn't have to think anymore." The attitudes which Flannery O'Connor satirizes are those of an age in which the intellectuals are positivists and the nonintellectuals are "positive thinkers." And, whether found in an inveterate rationalist such as the social worker Sheppard or in a self-righteous snob such as Ruby Turpin ("Revelation"), these attitudes signified to Flannery O'Connor a deathly incapacity for existence in depth which she considered the besetting affliction of the contemporary world.

Time and again in her stories, the spokesmen for a self-satisfied secularism run afoul of representatives of that third character-type mentioned above—the twisted, the guilt-ridden, the satan-possessed, and the God-haunted protagonists who might best be designated "criminal-compulsive." It is in the encounter of these representatives of opposing views of reality that Miss O'Connor characteristically dramatizes the "conflict between an attraction for the Holy and the disbelief in it" which is the gravitational center of her moral and artistic vision. And though it was the "criminal-compulsives" who earned her the reputation for gratuitous grotesquerie and violence, they play an indispensable role in this paradigmatic conflict: it is they who act as spiritual catalysts, administering the shock which awakens the positivists and the positive thinkers from their dream of a world made secure by superficial rationality or conventional goodness.

Because of the prominence of the three character-types, I frequently refer to them and to the conflicts generated among them, as exemplifying the typical O'Connor story. It will be self-evident, however, to readers at all familiar with her work that no such classification can be inclusive and, furthermore, that characters who seem to lend themselves to identification by type often prove far more complex than they initially appeared. Also, while there is a good deal of repetition of situation in O'Connor's fiction—especially in the short stories, where the widowed or divorced mother and the disaffected son or daughter are common features of the landscape—there is no single "O'Connor story" other than the drama of the fall of man which furnishes the background for everything she wrote.

The character-types appear most frequently in the tales collected in *A Good Man Is Hard to Find,* and in three of those I have selected for detailed analysis—"Good Country People," "A Circle in the Fire," and "A Good Man Is Hard to Find"—the conflict is rendered in pellucid and virtually paradigmatic form. In *Wise Blood* the self-satisfaction of positive thinking threatens the very bases of human life itself and finds its most eloquent spokesman in the landlady, Mrs. Flood, who is incapable of distinguishing between "being a saint" and "walling up cats." The fraudulent blind preacher, Asa Hawks, exemplifies some of the traits of the criminal-compulsive and plays a major role in bringing Hazel Motes to his moment of truth, while the latter character combines elements of the criminal-compulsive and the positivist (the philosophy which Haze at one point expounds can scarcely be mistaken as a parody of logical positivism). It is only in the second novel, however, that Miss O'Connor fully adapted the types to her longer fiction: Rayber, as I shall show, is a positivist *par excellence,* although the conflicting forces within his soul make inappropriate a simple, unqualified identification; and young Tarwater possesses a certain likeness to such criminal-compulsives as The Misfit and Rufus Johnson, though here also the designation would be misleading if not properly qualified.

The stories in *Everything That Rises Must Converge*

exemplify a somewhat different configuration of characters. There are, to be sure, still positivists (most notably Sheppard of "The Lame Shall Enter First"), just as there are positive thinkers (e.g., Mrs. May of "Greenleaf" and Ruby Turpin of "Revelation"). The mentally disturbed college student of the latter tale and the promiscuous, feline Sarah Ham of "The Comforts of Home" are not unlike some of the neurotic, criminal types of the earlier stories. And Rufus Johnson ("The Lame Shall Enter First"), is, of course, the prototypical O'Connor spokesman for spiritual crime, haunted by the devil while at the same time convinced of the truth of the Gospel. Yet in some of the finest of these tales—"A View of the Woods," "Parker's Back," "Everything That Rises Must Converge"—the conflicting views which in earlier stories had usually been expressed by different characters, are now lodged in the same individual. Hence, though in each of these stories there is a conflict between individuals, and the epiphany or "moment of grace" comes about as a consequence of that conflict, the antagonists are no longer criminals who appear without warning to destroy the bubble of self-sufficiency and smugness in which the protagonists are encased. They are instead persons close to the protagonist—a mother, a wife, a granddaughter—who embody one aspect of the protagonist's personality or who reflect a character trait so deeply repressed as to be almost atrophied. In "A View of the Woods," for example, there is a conflict within the protagonist, so subtle and so threatening to his idealized self-image that he can acknowledge it only as annoying disobedience in his granddaughter. When he attempts to punish her, however, he discovers an "enemy within" which destroys him even as he (inadvertently) kills its embodiment in the child. The stories in *Everything That Rises Must Converge* are characterized by such complexity of human

relations; and it is, I believe, Flannery O'Connor's growing perspicacity as a commentator upon human psychology, perhaps more than anything else, which her
final collection bears witness to.

Everything so far said about Flannery O'Connor
would tend to confirm the centrality of religious concerns in her fiction. As self-evident as this claim may
appear, it requires further discussion. One critic, who
offers original and provocative readings of O'Connor's
stories, strongly implies that her interpretations are "non-
religious"; and she quotes with approval Irving Howe's
statement, concerning the stories in *Everything That
Rises Must Converge*, that "[e]xcept for an occasional
phrase, which serves partly as a rhetorical signal that
more than ordinary verisimilitude is at stake, there are
no unavoidable pressures to consider these stories in a
strictly religious sense. They stand securely on their own,
as renderings and criticisms of human experience." [20]

Both the critic referred to, Josephine Hendin, and
Mr. Howe miss the point of Flannery O'Connor's basic
understanding of man and the transcendent reality of
which she believes his life to be a part. And they do so,
I think, because they share a fundamental confusion
about the nature of religion. The process of secularism
of the past four centuries has had two obvious and significant effects upon our understanding of religion and
our use of the word. First, religion has tended to become one among many human interests, a more or less
segregated activity of one's life, rather than the under-
girding structure giving meaning to the whole of life as
it was in former epochs. As a consequence, proponents
of religion frequently have been perceived as spiritual
public relations men, each promoting his special version
of the faith. In the realm of literary criticism one result
of the isolation of religion from the totality of human
affairs has been the attempt of some Christian critics to

use literature as a vehicle for propagation of the faith. Christ figures were uncovered in the most unlikely places, and Christian symbolism seemed to sprout in novels and plays as prolifically as heather on a Yorkshire moor.

On the other side—and this is the second effect—were those who increasingly came to view religion as a force alien to man's nature, at best a harmless pre-occupation of those with "spiritual" rather than temporal interests, at worst a crutch for those too weak to face reality without otherworldly support. Naturally, the literary critics among this group resented the use of literature for what they considered propagandistic ends. But they too have been the victims of the confusion occasioned by the secularization of life; with them the pendulum has sometimes swung so far in the opposite direction that metaphysical considerations have been judged a priori as extraneous to the critic's task.

The problem is one of definition. If religion is defined as a body of codified doctrine, with its attendant rituals and practices, then of course religion is likely to furnish the critic with a set of values and insights too systematized to illumine works of such complex beauty as "The Enduring Chill," "A View of the Woods" and "Good Country People." If, on the other hand, religion is defined in Kierkegaardian terms as "infinite passion" to realize the truth of one's existence or, in the language of Paul Tillich, as that "ultimate concern" which expresses itself in all human activity and is thus "the substance of culture," then clearly every serious work of art is susceptible of religious interpretation and the art of a Flannery O'Connor simply cannot be fully understood apart from it. For Flannery O'Connor, religion has meaning only to the degree that it bears upon what Howe finds at the heart of her stories—human experience. She and Tillich would surely have agreed that the more penetrating and profound the renderings and criticisms of that experience, the more "religious" the meanings which emerge. Repeatedly Miss O'Connor demonstrates—as do Melville, Dostoevsky, Faulkner, and Camus—that religious meaning emerges via human behavior and psychology, as men struggle with their experience in an effort to wrest from it some significance.

Very likely these matters will appear passé to many, yet the dilemma posed by the question, In what sense is Flannery O'Connor a religious writer, is serious and has not received the attention it deserves. Given the bifurcation in our understanding of religion to which I have alluded, it was only natural that Miss O'Connor should have proved an especially attractive author to critics themselves strongly committed to a religious view of man. Hence for a time O'Connor scholarship was dominated by those who looked upon this writer as primarily a spokesman for Christian orthodoxy, God's scourge, calling for repentance in the wilderness of contemporary American secularism. Only recently has there begun to appear a substantial body of critical opinion appreciative of the subtle ways in which her Christianity is transmuted in her art into something rather distinct from the religion of the received tradition. Mrs. Hendin's study, I suspect, reflects the impatience of "non-religious" critics with the narrowness and, at times, the shallowness of what, for lack of a better word, I shall call the "orthodox" readings of Flannery O'Connor's fiction. Although her book strikes me as often wrongheaded or even perverse in its denial of religious meaning where religious meaning so patently exists, she has performed a valuable service in stressing the existential/psychological dimensions of Miss O'Connor's characters, in effect "demythologizing" them, and thereby rendering them understandable in terms other than simply those of fall and redemption.

Yet the reaction has amounted to an overreaction. For the art of Flannery O'Connor is religious in two senses, and a criticism which attempts to interpret this art from an exclusively "non-religious" standpoint will inevitably distort it while failing to comprehend its deepest significance. In the most obvious sense of the word, Flannery O'Connor's art is religious because many of her characters consciously face the choice of Jesus or the devil, belief or nonbelief, faith òr apostasy. And even in stories where this appears not to be the case, e.g., "Everything That Rises Must Converge," "The Life You Save May Be Your Own," and "Greenleaf," symbol, allusion, and mythological motif coalesce to infuse them with a distinctly religious aura. In another and more basic sense Flannery O'Connor's art is religious, in that it endeavors to trace the figuration of that modern sensibility which permeates the literature of the West from Goethe and Carlyle through Dostoevsky and Baudelaire to Kafka and Camus and about which it is now a cliché to assert that it is a sensibility whose timbre ensues from the erosion of faith in the seventeenth and eighteenth centuries and the "death of God" in the nineteenth and twentieth centuries. Fundamentally, then, Flannery O'Connor is a religious writer not because the subject matter of her stories is "religious"—though explicitly or implicitly it almost always is—but because she has been occupied in all of her major fiction with the primary spiritual question of our era.

Two recent studies shed a good deal of light on the religious dimension of Flannery O'Connor's fiction and help correct, I believe, the impression of Hendin's book that psychological and theological interpretations are incompatible. In *The Christian Humanism of Flannery O'Connor* David Eggenschwiler propounds the thesis that, because she viewed man as an ontological totality whose health depends upon a proper relation to God, himself and his fellow men, Flannery O'Connor wrote about "wholeness and incompleteness," "unity and estrangement." [21] Drawing upon the religious psychology of the Danish philosopher Kierkegaard and the theology of Paul Tillich, Eggenschwiler makes a convincing case for O'Connor's fiction as a study of various forms of anxiety, obsession, "demonic" neurosis and despair. The advantage of this approach is that it permits discussion of a given character in psychological, sociological and theological terms simultaneously and frequently affords fresh insight into motives which are inadequately accounted for by any of these disciplines when used singly.

Briefly summarized, Eggenschwiler's argument is that, viewed from the perspective of Flannery O'Connor's Christian humanism, man is a synthesis of the divine and the earthly, that he is free and therefore experiences dread, and that, given this situation, he confronts two alternatives: to accept "himself, his limitations, his freedom, his responsibility, and his proper relation to God," which in essence means the acceptance of grace and faith. He may, however, choose to flee his relationship to God, thus "deny[ing] his essential self" and attempting "to escape dread through his own resources." This course of action is, to the Christian humanist, not only sinful but "ultimately self-defeating. Thus, turning from God is more than an ethical problem; it manifests itself in every aspect of man's being." [22] In Eggenschwiler's interpretation, therefore, the moral dilemmas of The Misfit or Hazel Motes are analyzed in psychological terms, but this in no way precludes discussion of these characters in theological and sociological categories also. Indeed, as Eggenschwiler's analysis demonstrates, only such a comprehensive intellectual framework is likely to do justice to the holistic view of man informing Flannery O'Connor's art.

The second volume which illumines the way in which

O'Connor's fiction is religious and at the same time profoundly true to human experience is *Invisible Parade* by Miles Orvell. An outstanding feature of this book is the critic's close attentiveness to the techniques of O'Connor's fiction which allows him to establish what has long been asserted but not always convincingly demonstrated: that O'Connor's finest tales display an elusiveness making impossible any effort to reduce them to a "theological formula. . . . Rather, they culminate in an image that is true dramatically, psychologically, and morally. With O'Connor, as with other writers of firm belief . . . , the unassailable dramatic image is closer to the vision than any doctrinal equivalent." [23] By careful and detailed examination of narrative voice, the idiosyncrasies of style, and the tension between surface meaning and symbolic meaning, Orvell shows how Flannery O'Connor was able to incarnate in her art a religious understanding of man which in no way interferes with, indeed, is integral to the reader's "discovery of the meaning latent in a given object or action." [24] In the process of symbolism as practiced by O'Connor, religious meaning and the meaning of ordinary human action co-inhere.

Having begun this chapter with some reflections on the mystery surrounding Miss O'Connor's life and work, I should like to conclude on a kindred note. Of contemporary American authors, Flannery O'Connor is surely one of the most controversial. She has been described as the most extreme Christian dualist since Dostoevsky,[25] and yet her perspective on the created universe appears to be unreservedly sacramentalist. Her fiction has been analyzed by a critic who views it as an American counterpart of the *nouveau roman* and as susceptible of nonreligious interpretation,[26] though Flannery O'Connor stated unequivocally that she wrote from "the standpoint of Christian orthodoxy." It has been claimed that O'Connor's characters suffer from limitations upon their freedom amounting to virtual psychological determinism or theological predestination, though she herself insisted that her characters are free and that "[f]reedom . . . is a mystery and one which a novel . . . can only be asked to deepen." [27] The present study makes no claim to final answers concerning the problems raised by such conflicting testimony. It will be enough if, in confronting the mystery of this remarkable woman and her truly extraordinary work, some small measure of illumination is afforded the inquiring reader. That the light thus produced will be no more than a flickering candle in a world of deepening shadows goes without saying.

2

Wise Blood

Between 1949 and 1952, except when illness made writing impossible, Flannery O'Connor worked steadily to complete a first novel. Using material from short stories written earlier, she apparently encountered a good deal of difficulty plotting a strategy for the final version. At one time it seemed as if Enoch Emery, not Hazel Motes, was to be the novel's protagonist; and Hazel himself underwent several transformations before becoming the fanatical anti-Jesus preacher of *Wise Blood* as finally published. Because of the nature of its composition, the novel has been said to suffer from a certain disjointedness of form and blurring of effect such as might be expected of a cut-and-paste effort. While there may be some validity to these criticisms, I hope to show that the inclusion of certain characters and incidents is aesthetically more appropriate than has generally been recognized.

Wise Blood is organized around a nexus of opposites: sin/innocence; animality/spirituality; commitment to nothing/commitment to evil; the deity of the *coincidentia oppositorium*/the god of debased theism; spiritual sight/spiritual blindness. The tension generated by these opposites functions to bring the protagonist Hazel Motes ever closer to a revelatory moment when the scales fall from his eyes and he achieves the vision of a mystic or saint. Once this still point in his frantic quest is reached, he blinds himself as he has no further use for the means of physical sight. At this juncture the final pair of opposites draws a minor character, and along with her, the reader, toward a dark tunnel where illumination is proffered but finally withheld from all but those capable of seeing with the eyes of faith.

In the resolution of the conflict between these pairs, attention is focused upon a central theme—mystery. A central theme of mystery might be expected from a writer who repeatedly maintained that the true meaning of a piece of fiction begins where such matters as credible character motivation and correct theology end. "The fiction writer," she once noted, "presents mystery through manners, grace through nature, but when he finishes there always has to be left over that sense of Mystery which cannot be accounted for by any human formula." [1]

Hazel Motes proclaims as a key doctrine of the Church Without Christ the proposition that "behind all [truths] there's only one truth and that is that there's no truth." [2] He is driven to this extreme nihilism by a haunting and half-acknowledged fear that there *is* one truth but not the one he preaches; namely, the truth of original sin. No matter how adamant his shrill insistence that fall and redemption are meaningless sounds, he cannot fully escape the knowledge hidden, as it were, in his blood. As Haze on one occasion expresses it, " 'There's no person a whoremonger who wasn't something worse first. That's not the sin, nor blasphemy. The sin came before them' " (45). It is this truth and its implications for him (Haze claims that he is "clean," not a sinner in need of redemption as his grandfather had declared) which Haze ultimately accepts.

In rejecting the truth of original sin, Haze unwittingly expresses the working philosophy of the city Taulkinham. For the people of Taulkinham subjectively experience themselves as innocent. " 'Every person that comes onto this earth,' " says the "artist-type" preacher Hoover Shoats, " 'is born sweet and full of love' " (83). In their own eyes "sweet" and uncorrupted, the inhabitants of the city can attend to the affairs of everyday with no spiritual disquietude. The mundane preoccupations of the day are sufficient thereunto. No one is exercised over Haze's blasphemy or his denials of Jesus and salvation, for each is secure in his complacent belief that, if anything resembling salvation is necessary, it is as easily accomplished as peeling a potato. Again it is Shoats who formulates the belief: " 'The unredeemed are redeeming theirselves. . . . Help yourself to salvation' " (91). Haze's preaching draws sarcastic remarks; Shoats's preaching draws crowds.

In such a setting those who exhibit anxiety concerning existential realities are considered freaks; when Hazel asks if anyone cares about the truth, a woman looks at him "as if he were in a booth at the fair" (82). Religion becomes indistinguishable from commercial enterprise (the fraudulent preacher Hawks asks, " 'Wouldn't you rather have me beg than preach' " [26] and Shoats wants to turn Haze's Church Without Christ into a dues-collecting association), and commercial enterprise becomes the *telos* of human existence. This is made explicit in the description of the city several nights after Haze's arrival: against the background of the sky which appears as a "vast construction work that involved the whole order of the universe and would take all time to complete," the people literally go about their business. "No one was paying any attention to the sky. The stores . . . stayed open . . . so that people could have an extra opportunity to see what was for sale" (24). On the street there are potato peelers for sale and Hawks and the salesman compete for the attention of prospective customers.

Despite their conviction of innocence, the people of

Taulkinham are hardly sweet and full of love; rather, they are acquisitive and unfriendly. The prevailing attitude toward property is represented in Haze's landlady, Mrs. Flood, who "felt justified in getting anything at all back that she could, money or anything else, as if she had once owned the earth and been dispossessed of it" (116). Unaware that she and her fellow citizens have indeed been dispossessed of their birthright by the fall, Mrs. Flood joins in the general scramble for material possessions—an unconscious attempt to regain Paradise.

Thus preoccupied they have little time or patience for others. Enoch Emery, admittedly a repulsive character not likely to attract friends, nevertheless accurately describes the city when he complains to Haze about his loneliness: " 'I been here two months,' " he says, " 'and I don't know nobody' " (30). At the FROSTY BOTTLE where Enoch has a milk shake before making his daily pilgrimage to the museum at the zoo where he works, a drunken waitress screams at Haze, " 'what do you think I care about any of you filthy boys?' " (53) Asa Hawks encourages Haze's attentions largely in order to unload on him his ugly daughter, Sabbath Lily. Haze encounters a dishonest and not overly-friendly used car salesman and, on another occasion, a cage in which, for the public's amusement, a hawk and a bear mutilate each other. When he discovers that Haze is driving without a license, a policeman destroys Haze's car and at the novel's end another police officer uses the dying Haze's skull as a practice target for his new billy club. The friendliest spot in town is reputed to be the bed of the prostitute, Mrs. Leora Watts, but Haze is received there by a loathsome cretin, whose company he can stand for no more than forty-eight hours.

While the average citizen's conviction of his innocent state creates an atmosphere characterized by cold indifference or violence, the near-total absence of genuine consciousness in Enoch Emery leads to animality. A satire on evolution and the American success story, Enoch's tale is also a farcical parody of mystical experience. A back-country rube who comes to the city seeking success and fame, Enoch is a Black Humor caricature of the image of man projected in the insurance ads—"THE young man of the future." Rather than "making it to the top," Enoch demonstrates one direction a fundamentally materialistic culture may take— downward toward the purely instinctual life of the animal world. Enoch's consciousness is subservient to mysterious subconscious promptings imaged as the "wise blood" he believes he has inherited from his daddy, a reversed reflection of the original sin Haze and Taulkinham believe they have *not* inherited. Impelled by his instincts while his consciousness sits and waits, Enoch lives a secret life among the animals and eventually "evolves" into a gorilla. The leap from humanity to animality, Enoch's story suggests, may be short indeed among a people for whom consciousness is an accident of the "onward march of progress" and spirituality is a joke.

Enoch's wise blood leads him to a "mystery," of which he alone has knowledge: a man, supposedly shrunken by "A-rabs," reposing in a glass-enclosed case at the museum. Enoch thus worships at the city's heart an effigy representing secular society's corruption and fraudulence (the "man" is really a sawdust-filled dummy). Convinced that his god is the "new jesus" of whom he has heard Hazel Motes preach, Enoch steals the mummy (it has been described as "an objectification of his deformed spirit") [3] in order to present it as an offering. First, however, he houses it in "a tabernacle-like cabinet which was meant to contain a slop-jar" (73) and which has undergone elaborate preparations as a receptacle for this sacred object in whose presence

Enoch speaks in a "church whisper." Subsequently he parts with his deformed spirit and, beginning a new phase of life, dons the gorilla suit of the famous Gonga. His god, he is convinced, "has finally rewarded" him (108). Thus does Enoch fulfill his destiny, enacting a ritual symbolizing the corruption of the human spirit in a time when men have lost an authentic image of humanity, as well as a vital, humanizing image of divinity.

Enoch's story, of course, is meant to be a parody of Hazel's and "helps define, by contrast, the sense in which Hazel is a Christian hero." [4] And, contrary to the opinion of several critics, the episodes involving Enoch do have an organic and functional relation to the main story line. Enoch's gift of the new jesus, for example, is a major cause propelling Haze toward recognition of the falsity of his anti-Jesus gospel. When Enoch brings the rain-soaked parcel to Haze's room, it is Sabbath Lily who receives the shriveled figure and, cradling it in her arms, calls it her "baby." Symbolically the new jesus is Hazel's child, sired by an apostle of nothingness upon the daughter of a fraud. By insisting upon his innocence and indirectly affirming the working philosophy of the city, Haze can produce only a grotesquerie such as Enoch's misshapened spirit. Seeing what he has begotten, Haze violently destroys it, for Enoch's new jesus is disturbingly unlike the truth he had sought through his blasphemy. " 'I don't want nothing but the truth!' " he says, " 'and what you see is the truth and I've seen it' " (103). " 'Preacher talk,' " replies Sabbath, and indeed it is, since precisely this desire for truth goads him eventually to abandon his denial of original sin and to embrace salvation.

Haze is driven toward his destiny by yet another twisted spirit, that of Sabbath's father, the "blind" preacher. Early in the novel Haze is taunted by Hawks, who claims that he can " 'hear the urge for Jesus in

[Haze's] voice' " (31); and through much of the remainder of the book Hawks acts upon Haze as a cause at once of fascination and irritation. On the occasion of their first meeting, Haze leans forward and stares "as if he were trying to see through [Hawks's] black glasses" (31), to penetrate, that is, the mystery of a man who has supposedly blinded himself to prove his faith and who loudly declares that Haze cannot " 'run away from Jesus' " because " 'Jesus is a fact' " (31–32). Thereafter Haze tends to define himself and to measure the success of his mission in terms of Hawks's response to his challenge. Though utterly repelled by Sabbath Lily, Haze determines to seduce her, expecting thereby to convince Hawks that he is truly dedicated to belief in nothing. Anticipating that the evangelist will make strenuous efforts to convert him, Haze is mystified by the frigid indifference with which Hawks receives the suggestion that his vocation should dictate greater concern for Haze's salvation.

It is to Hawks's black glasses, however, and to what he half-consciously suspects lurks behind them, that Haze is chiefly drawn. Having been given a spurious account of how Hawks came to be blind, Haze is obsessed with desire to know the details of the preacher's earlier sinful life and of his "conversion." Patently it is the ostensible strength of Hawks's belief which attracts Haze, but as this is symbolized by the preacher's eyes, Haze wants to see *"behind* the black glasses" (80). This impulse leads him to discover, after entering Hawks's room by stealth, that the blind man is a fraud. The discovery is a particularly unnerving one, for since Haze has conceived his relationship with Hawks as a contest of faiths, the fact that Hawks had lacked the courage to "blind himself for Jesus" is, for Haze, tantamount to a betrayal. Hawks, in other words, has become for Haze a symbol of steadfast faith, even if the object of that belief is, from Haze's standpoint, false. And since Haze's own faith is based upon a presumed affirmative answer to his earlier rhetorical questions—" 'Don't I know what exists and what don't? . . . Don't I have eyes in my head?' " (34)—this discovery, the culmination of numerous similar recognitions, that appearances deceive and that his eyes are unreliable, creates for Haze a crisis of belief.

For a full appreciation of the significance, both literal and symbolic, of Hawks in the conversion of Haze from a blasphemer to something resembling a penitent disciple of Jesus, close attention must be given to the false preacher's own terrifying encounter with Jesus. Years before the novel's action takes place, Hawks had promised to blind himself at a revival.

> He had preached for an hour on the blindness of Paul, working himself up until he saw himself struck blind by a Divine flash of lightning and, with courage enough then, he had thrust his hands into the bucket of wet lime and streaked them down his face; but he hadn't been able to let any of it get into his eyes. He had been possessed of as many devils as were necessary to do it, but at that instant, they disappeared, and he saw himself standing there as he was. He fancied Jesus, Who had expelled them, was standing there too, beckoning to him; and he had fled out of the tent into the alley and disappeared. (P. 65)

From this account there emerges a crucial fact: after Haze, Hawks is the most spiritually aware person in the novel. Alone among the secondary characters, Hawks knows that man is intended for some reality other than the gross sensuality and strident commercialism which pass for life in Taulkinham, and his despair is a consequence of his failure to grasp or be grasped by that reality. Thus Hawks preaches Christianity in order to undermine it, not simply to make money.

Whereas Hoover Shoats, the preacher of "up-to-date"

religion, is calculating but ludicrous in his forthright scheme to turn the Church Without Christ into a paying concern, Hawks, caught in a mesh of defiance and despair, is sinister, demonic. It is he, the small-time Lucifer (his first name may be derived from Azazel, leader of the rebellious archangels in the Book of Enoch; his surname connotes both his predatory nature and his fallen-angel status), who represents the real temptation to Haze to compromise his integrity. In escaping Jesus, Hawks has been converted to evil, and his mocking of that in which he once believed and his turning to a life of petty crime have a devastating effect upon his "disciple" Haze, bringing him close to Hawks's own despair. When he learns the preacher's true history, Haze appears ready to acknowledge the failure of his belief in nothing and to adopt evil as his truth. The temptation is poignantly represented in the seductive overtures of Sabbath Lily.

> "Listen," she said, . . . "from the minute I set eyes on you I said to myself, that's what I got to have. . . . That innocent look don't hide a thing, he's just pure filthy right down to the guts, like me. The only difference is I like being that way and he don't. Yes sir!" she said. "I like being that way, and I can teach you how to like it. Don't you want to learn how to like it?" (P. 92)

Haze's response, " 'Yeah . . . I want to,' " though uttered with total lack of enthusiasm, registers the degree to which knowledge of Hawks's untruth has undermined his confidence in the possibility of remaining converted "to nothing instead of to evil" (17).

Haze's determination to believe in nothing and to maintain his innocence is an outgrowth principally of his grandfather's fiery sermons. The old man had preached that Jesus would die ten million deaths even for a "mean sinful unthinking boy" such as Haze, and the youth's fear of the "soul hungry" Jesus leads to the conviction that "the way to avoid Jesus [is] to avoid sin" (16).

Several critics have shown how Haze's obsession with the unreality of sin is inextricably bound up also with his neurotic fear of sexuality in general and his un-resolved oedipal attachment to his severe, moralistic mother in particular.[5] And David Eggenschwiler has convincingly argued that it is fear of death, associated with Jesus the devourer, which haunts Hazel and ac-counts for his ambivalent attitude toward salvation.[6] In this respect the grandfather's role is crucial. Uncon-sciously identifying with the old man whom he re-sembles physically and in the dogmatic, inflexible quality of his preaching, Haze runs toward the destiny his grandfather had predicted even as he believes that he runs from it. Yet, so weighty is the burden of guilt and so powerful therefore the need to proclaim his in-nocence, that Haze must consciously reject redemption and fight Jesus. While Haze's statements that " 'there was no Fall because there was nothing to fall from and no Redemption because there was no Fall and no Judg-ment because there wasn't the first two' " are secular in tone and conform to the unexamined working principles of Taulkinham, for Haze they have the urgency of a reli-gion. The destiny the grandfather had set for him (which has its comic parallel in Enoch's "wise blood") Haze will ultimately discover to be inescapable.

Contrasted to Hazel's passionate commitment to truth is the heedlessness of the people of Taulkinham. Even they are not outright atheists, however, for some-where behind their perception of themselves as innocent there is hidden a god, a deity of their own creation rather like the one to whom Ruby Turpin ("Revelation") cries out, in an ecstatic burst of self-affirmation, " 'Thank you, Jesus, for making everything the way it is!' "[7] This is a debased form of Paul Tillich's "god of theism," it-self a religious view which makes of the deity one among many objects, albeit the highest. This deity's devotees are freed of annoying moral imperatives, having for the most part adopted the code of Hazel's landlady that " 'the time to enjoy yourself is now so long as you let others do the same' " (120). Among this god's followers, consciousness is accidental and thus responsibility for one's life and deeds is scarcely acknowledged.

Opposed to this attitude is awareness of original sin and its consequences, anxiety and death, as well as recognition of the possible validity of Hazel's assertion that behind all truths there is no Truth. For those who take seriously this understanding of existence, there appear to be two responses: to maintain one's innocence in the face of threatening absurdity, thereby intensifying the anxiety, or to acknowledge one's participation in the absurd. In the case of those with Christian ties, the latter choice dictates acceptance of a redeemer, either a redeemer who sanctifies particular things as holy and rejects all else, or a redeemer who embodies the *coincidentia oppositorium* and through whom all things are consecrated. The redeemer who sanctifies particulars is Hazel's grandfather's god—an escape from the absurd. The god to whom one surrenders that which he securely possesses in order to receive all, both positive and negative, is the god who ultimately redeems Hazel. However, since Hazel cannot help but associate redemption with acceptance of original sin and all it connotes, as preacher he must affirm his innocence by blaspheming. He resembles Camus's metaphysical rebel, who is "not definitely an atheist . . . but who is inevitably a blasphemer."[8]

But Haze is brought to acceptance of salvation only after the failure of one last attempt to find a city suitable for the establishment of the Church Without Christ. Having experienced the disillusionment of Hawks's betrayal and of Enoch's imbecilic distortion of his message, Haze kills the man hired (by Shoats) to impersonate him and prepares to leave Taulkinham. Now his philosophy exhibits an even more radical renunciation of his destiny. Since affirming himself against negation (the absurd) implied some degree of acceptance of negation, he is now moved to deny everything intangible—including that on the basis of which he had been able to affirm himself: "He said it was not right to believe anything you couldn't see or hold in your hand or test with your teeth. He said he had . . . believed in blasphemy as the way to salvation, but that you couldn't even believe in that because then you were believing in something to blaspheme" (112). But he immediately begins to blaspheme—quite violently—thus indicating the desperate extremity of his spiritual state as well as the bankruptcy of his logic. Like Melville's Ahab, he must have something to rage against in order to be. Only when an official representative of the city dispossesses him of his car—the leaking rattletrap symbolizing the secular alternative to salvation—does Haze perceive the true significance of his rejection of the possibility even of repudiating redemption. Once the something he had affirmed is taken from him, he has nothing left as defense against the absurd. He is engulfed by it and then, at last, he can accept the truth of original sin. His vision is of pure emptiness, of "the entire distance that extended from his eyes to the blank gray sky that went on, depth after depth, into space" (113–14). The sky is the same one that had contained a vast construction work, but now it seems to contain nothing at all, nothing to rebel against, nothing to rest in. It is similar to the single truth Hazel had expounded, that beyond the relative truths of men there is no truth at all, that ultimate truth is emptiness. In the midst of this vast nothing, of this dark night of the soul, he accepts redemption.

Exactly what it is that Haze now moves toward (he blinds himself and undergoes a penance of severe self-torture in order "to pay"), it is impossible to specify: there is left over, after we have examined various human causes for his behavior, "that sense of Mystery which cannot be accounted for by any human formula." At this point the final pair of opposites comes into play and through the character of Mrs. Flood the reader is assisted in gaining perspective on Haze's action even if he can not fully sanction it. Mrs. Flood is an early specimen of the genus "positive thinker," and in the novel's final chapter the point of view is largely hers. It is she who comments on the foolishness of Haze's self-blinding ("if she had felt that bad . . . she would simply have put her head in an oven" [114]) and who subsequently concludes that he is a madman—significantly, *after* she learns that he is placing his "left over" money in the wastebasket. It has been argued that in giving the final word, as it were, to so philistine a creature as Mrs. Flood, Flannery O'Connor offers the reader no alternative but to grant approval to the morbid and Manichaean form of salvation dictated by Haze's fundamentalist background.[9] Perhaps this is so. Certainly no thoughtful reader wishes to be identified with the "sensible" Mrs. Flood, whose views reflect so fully that spiritual wasteland Taulkinham. Yet this interpretation makes too little, I think, of the changes which Mrs. Flood experiences under the influence of Haze's grim self-mortification. A woman addicted to creature comforts and totally at home in the ordinary and the everyday, Mrs. Flood is moved by Haze's example from seemingly imperturbable complacency to an anxious desire to know his "secret." As she attempts to follow the "pinpoint of light" which she imagines Haze at the end to have become, she is brought to the threshold of mystery. And while she is stopped there, and there is no hint that she will ever move beyond—into the mystery, as Haze has done—the final impression left with the reader is that Mrs. Flood has been granted a spiritual awakening which, no matter how limited, in a sense validates Haze's own journey (as she had earlier imagined it) "backwards to Bethlehem" (119). Then she had attempted to visualize what was going on in his head, but all she could conjure up was a vision of "the whole black world in his head and his head bigger than the world, his head big enough to include the sky and planets and whatever was or had been or would be" (119). It is, of course, a vision of eternity, precisely that "vast construction work that involved the whole order of the universe and would take all time to complete," and of which the other people of the secular city have lost all recollection.

In her essay on "Catholic Novelists and Their Readers," Miss O'Connor asserts that "the Catholic writer often finds himself writing in and for a world that is unprepared and unwilling to see the meaning of life as he sees it." As a consequence, "he may resort to violent literary means to get his vision across to a hostile audience." [10] *Wise Blood*, it may safely be assumed, was written for "a hostile audience" and is therefore filled with violence. Surely the author must have felt the inadequacy of Haze's salvation, the achievement of which depends so heavily upon his perpetration of violence upon others and the consummation of which entails masochistic violence inflicted upon himself. Yet determined as she was to convey with the greatest force possible the reality of a mysterious deity who eludes the categories of human thought and the limitations of human ethics, and before whom human things are as nothing, she could hardly have wished to end *Wise Blood* with a converted Hazel Motes preaching Jesus to the self-sufficient and indifferent masses of Taulkinham. (Even in *The Violent Bear It Away* she shied away from such a conclusion.) In the world of *Wise Blood,* where insipidity, duplicity, and bad faith are so pervasive as to threaten the very concept of truth, Flannery O'Connor appears to say that obsession, with its concomitant violence and crime, is perhaps a necessary instrument in man's quest for meaning and salvation. If a Mrs. Flood can be brought to a visionary apprehension of a "secret" dimension of reality which her spiritual myopia has heretofore left undisclosed, what may not be possible, Miss O'Connor would seem to be asking, for the reader perhaps more responsive to "the violence of a single-minded respect for the truth." [11]

3

A Good Man Is Hard to Find

If the achievement of *Wise Blood* left any question as to the seriousness of Flannery O'Connor's literary ambitions, the publication three years later of *A Good Man Is Hard to Find* (1955) went far in dispelling all lingering doubts. The title alone, with its resonances of multiple levels of meaning and its evocation of problems of an existential and religious nature, was enough to suggest that here was no ordinary potpourri of "adult" bedtime reading. For the most part, the book was better understood than *Wise Blood* had been, the response of reviewers and critics alike being generally appreciative. In a letter to the Fitzgeralds, to whom the volume was dedicated, the author described the collection as "nine stories about original sin" [1] (the actual number is ten). But if the intended theme of these stories was original sin, the subject matter and situations through which the theme was explored were extremely varied and indicated that, though her syntax might have been "one-cylinder," as she herself confessed, Flannery O'Connor's instinct for the explosive and revealing human experience suffered from no such limitation.

A large measure of the book's initial appeal lay in Miss O'Connor's adroit handling of character, for the volume contains abundant testimony to her talent for portraying an image of man firmly planted in her native

Georgia soil, evincing all the nuances of locale and custom with which she was most familiar, yet so imprinted with the tragic/comic destiny of Man as to be of universal significance. Permeating the entire collection was a stark mood of alienation. No one in these stories has escaped the existential consequence of the fall—estrangement. Those who believe they know themselves best discover that they have been living with a stranger. Those who appear to be innocent and friendly strangers as often as not turn out to be avatars of the devil. So intense is the estrangement and so all-pervasive, that it almost inevitably erupts in violence, and the violence, while frequently ending in the death of one or more of the characters, just as frequently leads to an epiphany or what Flannery O'Connor preferred to call the "moment of grace."

Several recurrent themes give to the collection its unmistakable O'Connor imprint: the already-mentioned violence; a sense of violation and outrage as omnipresent here as it is in Faulkner; moral and ethical confusion resulting from a superficial understanding of the nature of good and evil; the ontological privation of man cut off from the source of his being; his self-deceptive belief in his "innocence" or in the efficacy of works to bring about salvation; and the action of God's grace through creatures with demonic traits.

Miss O'Connor's characters run the gamut from a neglected, unloved child ("The River") to an ancient Civil War veteran ("A Late Encounter with the Enemy") and include a precocious preadolescent seeking sainthood and learning the mysteries of sexuality ("A Temple of the Holy Ghost"), and a Polish emigrant who dies because he inadvertently threatens to subvert the pattern of race relations in a land whose ways he does not understand ("The Displaced Person"). The three character types described earlier appear with unusual frequency—the positivist, the positive thinker, and the criminal-compulsive; and in this collection they are first seen full-blown and interacting within the same story.

In "Good Country People," for example, there appears a lively specimen of the criminal-compulsive, as well as a family relationship in which a positivist and a positive thinker prominently figure. Joy and her mother, Mrs. Hopewell, make up the prime configuration: the disaffected young rebel, more often than not cynical but most certainly imbued with pretentions to intellectualism, and typically alienated from the smug, uncritical parent; the parent, self-satisfied, optimistic, endowed with what seems an inexhaustible repertoire of platitudes of a moral or religious cast but actually dedicated to philistine values and the profit motive. Mrs. Hopewell, as her name implies, is a regular subscriber to the "life can be beautiful" philosophy. In contrast to her daughter Joy, whose distinguishing features are a nasty disposition and an artificial leg, Mrs. Hopewell staunchly maintains that "people who looked on the bright side of things would be beautiful even if they were not" (247). Joy is brilliant but cynical, and derives a perverse pleasure from affronting her mother's flaccid optimism with a look expressing her characteristic emotion of outrage. Joy's perversity prompts her to adopt the name Hulga, the most unpleasant sound she can think of; and she complements the ugliness of her new name with a sullen rudeness of behavior to her mother and the latter's "companion," Mrs. Freeman. A self-styled atheist, with a Ph.D. in philosophy, Hulga is rendered almost physically ill by the intensity of her contempt for what she considers the utterly fatuous and banal world of her mother, who appears incapable of thought more profound than the sentiment that " 'good country people' " —of whom, in her opinion, Mrs. Freeman is a notable example—are " 'the salt of the earth' " (250).

Into this world there suddenly intrudes another representative of "good country people" (or so Mrs. Hopewell assumes), an itinerant Bible salesman named Manley Pointer. Appearing to be the very essence of innocence and naïveté, Pointer has little difficulty ingratiating himself with Mrs. Hopewell and matches her clichés with unctious pieties about " 'Christian service' " and " 'real honest people,' " nowadays only to be found " 'way out in the country.' "

As attracted to his apparent innocence as she is repelled by his platitudinous religious attitudes, and finding a common identity with Manley (they both have a not unsymbolic "heart condition"), Joy agrees to accompany the boy on a picnic. Lying in bed that evening Hulga anticipates the role she will play in the Bible saleman's "education."

> She imagined that the two of them walked on the place until they came to the storage barn beyond the two back fields and there, she imagined, that things came to such a pass that she very easily seduced him and that then, of course, she had to reckon with his remorse. True genius can get an idea across even to an inferior mind. She imagined that she took his remorse in hand and changed it into a deeper understanding of life. She took all his shame away and turned it into something useful. (P. 255)

As the condescending Eve, Hulga will lead Manley into knowledge—not, however, knowledge of good and evil, but a more austere perception that both good and evil are illusions. " 'I'm one of those people who see *through* to nothing,' " she tells him. " 'We are all damned . . . but some of us have taken off our blindfolds and see that there's nothing to see. It's a kind of salvation' " (258).

The denouement of the story is at once pathetic and ironically comic. Hulga and the salesman do indeed enter the storage barn and climb to the loft, but here,

Hulga's coldly calculating intelligence forsakes her completely. Earlier, while walking in the woods, she had allowed Pointer to kiss her, and at that time her mind was described as "clear and detached and ironic . . . regarding him from a great distance, with amusement but with pity." (256). In the barn she kisses him with seeming passion, although "her mind" all the while "never stopped or lost itself for a second to her feelings" (258). Pointer declares his love for Hulga and demands that she permit him to remove her artificial leg as proof of her love for him. This she refuses to do until he announces that it is her artificial leg which fascinates him. " 'It's what makes you different. You ain't like anybody else' " (259). And this, of course, is Hulga's undoing, literally and figuratively. Allowing her secret pride in her "difference" and her submerged self-pity to becloud her "clear and detached and ironic" vision, Hulga gives Pointer her leg and immediately loses that mastery over him on which her entire scheme depends. Feeling himself now in command, Pointer takes from his valise a hollowed-out Bible containing a small whiskey flask, a pack of pornographic cards, and a box of contraceptives. Hulga the cynic, the believer in nothing, is at first too startled to speak; when at last she does respond, it is in a voice described as "almost pleading": " 'Aren't you,' she murmured, 'aren't you just good country people?' " Pointer answers with a surly " 'Yeah . . . but it ain't held me back none' " (260); and when Hulga complains furiously that he's " 'a perfect Christian,' " i.e., a thoroughly hypocritical one, this young man whom she has assumed to be the epitome of "real innocence" disabuses her once and for all of *her* illusions: " 'I hope you don't think,' he said in a lofty indignant tone, 'that I believe in that crap! I may sell Bibles but I know which end is up and I wasn't born yesterday' " (261). As he disappears out of the loft,

with Hulga's leg safely ensconced in his valise, along
with souvenirs of other similar escapades, Pointer de-
livers his *coup de grâce:* " 'And I'll tell you another
thing, Hulga . . . you ain't so smart. I been believing
in nothing ever since I was born!' " (261). While Hulga
remains in the barn, her face "churning" with anger,
Mrs. Hopewell and Mrs. Freeman watch Pointer cross-
ing over the meadow to the highway. Mrs. Hopewell,
with splendid unconscious irony, refers to the Bible
salesman as "so simple" and adds, typically, " 'but I
guess the world would be better off if we were all that
simple.' " Mrs. Freeman's reply reveals her essential
character: " 'Some can't be that simple . . . I know I
never could' " (261).

One critic has maintained that the story continues
past its natural conclusion at the moment of "symbolic
defloration," [2] but Flannery O'Connor had, I think,
good reasons for giving the last word to Mrs. Freeman.
For the wife of the hired hand plays a significant role
in the story's thematic development. The long first
paragraph is devoted to her; and her interest in physical
deformities and monstrosities, developed in some detail
in the narrative, is either integral to the story's purpose
or the tale contains not one superfluous paragraph but
two—the last *and* the first. Both paragraphs, however,
are necessary, for the story largely concerns deforma-
tions of the body which reflect corruptions of the spirit;
and this theme is advanced just as surely, though more
subtly, through the relation of Hulga and Mrs. Freeman
as it is through that of Hulga and Pointer. Mrs. Freeman is *free* of the illusions which blind both mother
and daughter, seeing more deeply into Hulga's soul than
does Mrs. Hopewell, who is too preoccupied with efforts
to improve "the child's" disposition to attempt to understand her.

After the ritual name changing, Mrs. Hopewell continues to call her "child" Joy, but in time Mrs. Freeman begins to use the adopted name, thereby causing Hulga extreme annoyance, since in so doing she invades the private domain bounded by the name, the self-created self it is meant to designate, and the artificial leg which is symbolic of the entire psychic structure. When Mrs. Freeman treads profanely upon this sacred soil, Hulga is inclined to "scowl and redden as if her privacy had been intruded upon."

> She considered the name her personal affair. . . . One of her major triumphs was that her mother had not been able to turn her dust into Joy, but the greatest one was that she had been able to turn it herself into Hulga. However, Mrs. Freeman's relish for using the name only irritated her. It was as if Mrs. Freeman's *beady steel-pointed eyes had penetrated far enough behind her face to reach some secret fact* [emphasis added]. (P. 246)

Mrs. Freeman, whose attraction to "the details of secret infections, hidden deformities, assaults upon children" is boundless, has in truth discovered a "secret fact" and the fact has much to do with the significance for Hulga of the artificial leg. Mrs. Freeman is fascinated by the leg, but it is a "secret infection," spiritual and psychological in nature, of which the leg provides intimations, toward which her eyes inevitably gravitate.

It is, of course, not only Mrs. Freeman who is fascinated by the leg but also Pointer, as is made clear through numerous "signals," one being the first question he asks Hulga on the day of the picnic: " 'Where does your wooden leg join on?' " (256) Earlier, when he had engaged Hulga in conversation preparatory to asking her for the date, Pointer had gazed at her "with open curiosity, like a child watching a new fantastic animal at the zoo. . . . His gaze seemed somehow familiar but she could not think where she had been regarded with it before" (254). The gaze *is* familiar since it is merely a masculine version of Mrs. Freeman's concentrated and penetrating stare, the similarity made unmistakable when Pointer's eyes, after he has successfully separated Hulga from her leg and is casting compulsive glances at it, are described as "like two steel spikes" (260). As Pointer, near the story's end, is to expose Hulga's pretenses, so Mrs. Freeman has already done earlier. Her "beady steel-pointed eyes" have discerned that Hulga is not what she would like to be taken for—a tough-minded, unsentimental, sophisticated materialist. Her comment, after spying Pointer and Hulga talking together following the salesman's initial appearance at the Hopewell farm, that " '[s]ome people are more alike than others' " (253), infuriates Hulga, for it indicates that Mrs. Freeman has taken the true measure of Hulga's supposed cynical detachment from all normal human relations.

On the level of conscious awareness Hulga believes that she allows Pointer a limited degree of intimacy because his innocence will afford her a rare opportunity to be the "professor" of atheism and nothingness which her physical disabilities generally preclude. Actually Hulga longs for the warmth of human contact, longs in fact for a relationship in which she can play the dual roles of protected child and adoring mother. Though hardly aware of her hunger, Hulga covets an innocence identical to that which she imagines to be fundamental to Pointer's character. The true "secret fact" is that Hulga desires a return to Eden, to the life of play which constitutes the world of childhood, a prelapsarian existence of unity and uninterrupted mutuality. Consciously wishing to be Eve of the temptation, unconsciously she seeks the condition of Eve before the fall. This is one of the story's great ironies; another is that Mrs. Hopewell, for all her obtuseness, is correct: Joy-Hulga *is* a child.

That this is the case becomes evident in the barn loft when Hulga surrenders to Pointer's blandishments. The following description of Hulga's highly emotive reaction to Pointer's comment that " 'You ain't like anybody else' " is crucial for a just appraisal of her self-deceptive pose as the aloof, self-contained, rationalistic intellectual.

> She sat staring at him. There was nothing about her face or her round freezing-blue eyes to indicate that this had moved her; but she felt as if her heart had stopped and left her mind to pump her blood. She decided that for the first time in her life she was face to face with real innocence. This boy, with an instinct that came from beyond wisdom, had touched the truth about her. When after a minute, she said in a hoarse high voice, "All right," it was like surrendering to him completely. It was like losing her own life and finding it again, miraculously, in his. (P. 259)

The final lines are remarkable not only for the suggestion of parody of the Gospel parable, which, in fact, Pointer had recited the previous day in the Hopewell sitting room (the devil quoting scripture!), but also for the hints they give concerning Hulga's "secret." On several previous occasions Hulga has mentioned "salvation," the intended meaning of the word always being her enlightened view of the reality of Nothing. Here a more powerful and more authentic impulse toward salvation is manifest; a salvation whose terms—surrender, losing one's life, finding it again miraculously in the life of another and thereby experiencing spiritual resurrection—parallel exactly the scheme of Christian redemption. Yet it is not Christian redemption for which Hulga yearns but rather a state of being which makes such redemption unnecessary. To be reborn into innocence, to shed the weight of consciousness and pain which life in the world entails—it is salvation of this sort which is Hulga's deepest desire.

Numerous details might be cited to support this conclusion. When, for instance, Hulga kisses Pointer she does so "as if she were trying to draw all the breath out of him" (258). But his breath is described as "clear and sweet like a child's" and his kisses are "sticky like a child's"; since breath is a traditional symbol of spirit, it would appear that Hulga compulsively attempts to draw into herself Pointer's supposedly "clear and sweet" spirit. When Pointer mumbles incoherently of his love, Hulga's role as the mother redeemed by the purity of her child is intimated by the boy's murmurings, which are "like the sleepy fretting of a child being put to sleep by his mother" (258). That the relationship as she comes to imagine it is one of childhood playfulness becomes more evident when Manley practices taking off the leg and replacing it, finally exclaiming, with an expression resembling that of a delighted child: " 'See!' . . . 'Now I can do it myself!' " (259) Hulga's total immersion in this image of life-as-endless-play is expressed most vividly in her fantasy of "run [ing] away" with Pointer to an Edenic world where each day would end with Pointer's loving removal of the leg and each new day begin with his putting it "back on again." In such a world, Hulga is both mother and child, protectress and protected, lover and beloved. The roles unite because in this world, created out of Hulga's profoundest longing, all of the antinomies, the vexing contradictions, the soul-taxing dichotomies of real existence have been overcome. Hulga's dream is, finally, a dream of human wholeness and for a few moments the reader is inclined to share her vision. Yet quickly it is shown to be the very essence of Hulga's sin because of her desire to circumvent, without the suffering which redemption always entails, what the author considers the primary datum of the human situation—the fallen nature of man.

This fantasy, the culmination of Hulga's progressive revelation of her hidden self, is followed immediately by

Pointer's disclosure of his true character. The explosive fury provoked in Hulga is thus to be accounted for not only as her predictable indignation at having been tricked by the "perfect Christian" who turns out to be a lewd, voyeuristic fraud, but more fundamentally as pure outrage occasioned by the betrayal of one whom she has come to consider a destined soulmate. The depth of Hulga's need for something in which she can believe and trust is illustrated by her pained cry that Pointer is " 'just like them all [i.e., the fraudulent "perfect Christians" she has known]—say one thing and do another' " (261). Though superficially she resembles the rationalist Sheppard, Hulga's more profound kinship is with a character such as Hazel Motes, in that both seek innocence and truth in a world which knows little of either.

Hulga's dream of running away to a world more capable of fulfilling the elemental human desire for unity and *joy* (it is, of course, her Joy-identity which is primary and which seeks realization in her dream) indicates how badly scarred she has been by life itself, not merely by the loss of the leg. The lost leg is an objective correlative of the lost unity of childhood, just as the wooden leg is an objective correlative of the pretended cynicism which is Hulga's self-protective response to adult reality. (It can hardly be a matter of chance that the key event in her fantasy of joyful existence is the removal of her leg by the childlike Pointer.) Self-exiled from the "grown-up" world whose fraudulence and cant she detests and cut off from the childhood world of playful bliss of which she has only unconscious or preconscious memories, Joy-Hulga dangles in limbo.

"Good Country People" gives us an admirable example of that depth of character which eludes easy classification. A typology of the sort I have suggested is frequently useful for character analysis and thematic interpretation. For example, Pointer's status as a "criminal-compulsive" is clear. But it is unwise to read this body of fiction exclusively in terms of categories of character type, whether those I have proposed or some others. This is a conclusion which will become clearer in the discussion of *The Violent Bear It Away*; but "Good Country People" demonstrates the point with sufficient force to establish its validity.

Yet it *is* possible at the most obvious level of interpretation to say that Flannery O'Connor's intention in the dramatic encounter of Hulga and Pointer appears to be the exposure of a facile, superficial, and finally sentimental nihilism as it meets head-on a nihilism which, while entirely nonintellectual, is nonetheless real and implacable. Seen from this vantage point, Hulga's mean-spirited perversity proves merely a façade; and when she is compelled to acknowledge the existence of perversity profounder than her own—more a part of the true scheme of things, because partaking more fully of evil as a metaphysical reality—she responds with incredulity, shock, and impotent outrage. Thus is portrayed Hulga the positivist, experiencing the shock of evil which initiates her into what Hawthorne called "the sinful brotherhood of mankind." In this respect Hulga is like many another O'Connor character who experiences a sense of utter helplessness as he is made to confront a dimension of reality whose very existence his positivism or his positive thinking has prompted him to deny or ignore.

It might be well to present briefly another illustration of this shock technique to indicate its pervasiveness. "A Circle in the Fire" is the story of Mrs. Cope, who, while paying lip service to some vague notion of divine providence, actually worships at the altar of her own resourcefulness. " 'I have the best kept place in the

county,'" she declares. "'Because I work. I've had to
work to save this place and work to keep it'" (217).
Like Hulga, Mrs. Cope has created her own world and
believes it inviolate: "'I don't let anything get ahead
of me and I'm not always looking for trouble. I take
it as it comes.'" Mrs. Pritchard, the hired hand's wife,
who preaches hard to Mrs. Cope, somewhat in the
manner of a Greek chorus, begins a reply: "'If it all
comes at oncet sometime'" but is cut short by Mrs.
Cope's self-assured retort, "'It doesn't all come at
once.'" Mrs. Pritchard's response, "'Well, if it ever
did . . . it wouldn't be nothing you could do but fling
up your hands'" (218), provides the note of Christian
tragedy in which is enacted the fall of a self-satisfied
protagonist from prosperity to misfortune.

The Eden which Mrs. Cope has fashioned with her
hands (early in the story she pulls at "weeds and nut
grass as if they were an evil sent directly by the devil
to destroy the place") is promptly invaded by evil
forces far less tractable than the trouble which she has
heretofore been able to "take as it comes." For down
the road to her farm come three teen-age boys from
Atlanta, one of whom, a bespectacled and hollow-
chested youth named Powell, had lived on her place as
a child. Powell and his companions are the very in-
carnation of unprovoked, irrational malignity, as Mrs.
Pritchard is quick to discern. ("'You take a boy thir-
teen year old is equal in meanness to a man twict his
age. It's no telling what he'll think up to do. You never
know where he'll strike next'" [225].) But Mrs. Cope
is too blinded by her positive view of human nature
and her unshakable confidence in her own competence
to take Mrs. Pritchard's warning seriously. When one
of the boys tells her that Powell once locked a small
brother in a box and set fire to it, the only response she
is capable of is a cheerful and incredulous inanity:

" 'I'm sure Powell wouldn't do a thing like that' "
(223). As these young delinquents gratuitously commit first one and then another act of destruction or
perversity, she comes ever closer to realizing the truth
of Mrs. Pritchard's oft-repeated litany, " 'There ain't
a thing you can do about it.' " But still she insists on
responding with sweet reasonableness rather than the
direct action proposed by her twelve-year-old daughter.

Condescending to what she considers Mrs. Pritchard's
superstitious mind and proud of her own rationality,
Mrs. Cope goes blindly to her tryst with fate. For, on
the next morning, Powell and his friends set fire to
Mrs. Cope's most treasured possession—her woods. As
the first licks its way among the trees and the boys
whoop and dance Indian-fashion, Mrs. Cope, for once
stunned and impotent, stands silent before the reality
of evil, at last utterly incontrovertible. Even the child,
who is portrayed throughout the story as a good deal
wiser than her mother, feels "weighed down with some
new unplaced misery" (231). And, as she stands beside
her mother, staring "up at her face as if she had never
seen it before," she beholds there the image of that new
misery which she herself has just experienced.

Only by means of the shock of evil, the inescapable
confrontation with an irrational and intractable malignancy, is Mrs. Cope brought to awareness of her participation in the common fate of mankind. For the
child the recognition seems to bring its own moment of
grace, for, as she stands "taut, listening," she hears
faintly "in the distance a few wild high shrieks of joy,
as if the prophets were dancing in the fiery furnace, in
the circle the angel had cleared for them" (232). Literally, of course, she hears only the war whoops of
Powell and his fellow incendiaries, but the figure suggests that the child's imagination, being more ingenuous
and freer of self-delusion than her mother's, is able to

apprehend something redemptive even in the heart of catastrophe. But, before the mystery of human depravity, Mrs. Cope is simply stunned, "as if she had had a searchlight thrown upon her in the middle of the night" (225). This is Mrs. Cope's moment of grace, as austere and wounding as Hulga's, the recognition that her vision has been incomplete, that she can no longer hide from "the terrible speed of mercy" which, in the words of The Violent Bear It Away, "burns clean."

"A Circle in the Fire" focuses directly upon the delusions of the positive thinker; "Good Country People" goes one step further in exposing the sterile rationalism of the age. "A Good Man Is Hard to Find," as we shall see, invites attention to the third character type, the criminal-compulsive. In this, the title story, the shock of evil is more terrifying than in the two stories analyzed above. In this tale a young father is about to take his wife and children and the children's grandmother from their home in Georgia on a vacation to Florida. While the entire family is portrayed as vapid and incorrigibly philistine, the grandmother especially displays a soul so empty that it seems to reverberate with the echoes of her own incessant chatter. Smug, self-willed and obsessed with breeding and "good blood," she is determined that the family go to East Tennessee to visit relatives, rather than to Florida. When attempts to persuade her son, Bailey, to alter his plans prove unavailing, she insists that at least they turn off the highway to investigate an old mansion she had visited as a child. And, in a deliberate effort to excite the children, she fabricates a story of a hidden panel and lost treasure. Grumbling avowals to make this concession the last, Bailey acquiesces.

Minutes later, the old lady remembers with a start that the house they are searching for is in Tennessee rather than in Georgia. Now utterly disoriented, she

kicks over a valise, thus allowing her cat—hidden in a
basket beneath—to spring onto Bailey's shoulder. In
the ensuing commotion, Bailey loses control of the car,
which bounces off the road and overturns. As the family
extricate themselves from the wreck, they see, on the
road above, another automobile from which emerge
three escaped convicts. The grandmother, with her
unerring instinct for trouble, blurts out the identity of
the group's leader, The Misfit, whose picture she has
seen in a newspaper.

From here the story moves with Sophoclean swiftness
to its catastrophe: first Bailey and the boy, then the
mother and her daughter, are led off to the woods and
shot. Only the grandmother, rendered almost insane by
fear, is left to confront the philosophical psychopath,
The Misfit, a man who finds no pleasure in life but
"meanness" and who claims that " 'Jesus thown everything off balance' " (142). Like Mrs. Hopewell in her
habitual refusal to recognize that there is more to life
than "the bright side of things," the grandmother faces
The Misfit with nothing more than a mouthful of
banalities (" 'You're not a bit common! I just know
you're a good man' ") which serve to reinforce our
already established impression that, for her, goodness
and gentility are merely social counters to be employed
whenever expediency demands it. When The Misfit
declares that he has assumed his name because he
can not make " 'what all I done wrong fit what all I
gone through in punishment' " (142), she responds by
suggesting that perhaps he was only mistakenly committed to the penitentiary. But, like her other inane
remarks, this statement demonstrates how unable she
is to comprehend either The Misfit's belief that everything was once "thown off balance" or the mystery of
evil which he himself ambiguously embodies. That the
world itself might be awry, that injustice might be a

permanent and irreducible component of human existence, that sham gentility offers no "safe conduct"
through this life—all of these intimations, as they flood
her consciousness, leave her traumatized and panting,
in a swoon of disbelief.

At last, faced with imminent death, the old lady
grasps at the only supports available to her: conventional piety, her faith in good breeding, and the commercial ideals of the society she so pathetically represents. Having tried to tell The Misfit that he must pray
and having succeeded only in speaking the name of
Jesus more as a curse than as a prayer, she makes one
last effort to save herself: " 'Jesus! . . . You've got
good blood! I know you wouldn't shoot a lady! I know
you come from nice people! Pray! Jesus, you ought not
to shoot a lady. I'll give you all the money I've got' "
(142).

Moments later, amidst The Misfit's pitiable com-
plaints of the injustice done him in the denial of
absolute certainty concerning Jesus and the dead He is
reported to have raised, the grandmother's vision clears.
Stretching out her hand, she touches him and mur-
murs, " 'Why you're one of my babies. . . . one of my
own children' " (143). Commentators have often noted
that in rejecting the old lady's proffered sympathy (it
is at this point that he shoots her), The Misfit turns
his back on the possibility of redemption; and the
grandmother's gesture has frequently been cited as her
"moment of grace." Not always, however, has it been
made clear why this is the case, since the action might
conceivably be interpreted as one more attempt on the
grandmother's part to deflect The Misfit's violence from
herself. Miss O'Connor herself supplied the explanation
when, in discussing this story with students at Hollins
College, she pointed out that in her short fiction there
is usually "some gesture of a character that is unlike any

other in the story," one that is "both in character and
beyond character," that suggests "both the world and
eternity," that "somehow [makes] contact with mystery." [3] Such a gesture is the grandmother's, who, as
Miss O'Connor goes on to explain, recognizes briefly
and dimly that she and The Misfit are bound together
by the mystery of life and death, a mystery which, until
this moment of extremity, she has been able to ignore.
Given this view of the grandmother's action, it is understandable that the author should describe her as the
story's heroine.

Until the instant when her "head clears," however,
it is the grandmother's inauthenticity which is being
judged by The Misfit's honesty and spirituality, perverse
though they be. As the title suggests, the theme of this
story is the question, What constitutes a good man?
Thus, the grandmother's insistence that The Misfit is an
example of this rare species is both ironically appropriate and grotesquely inappropriate. The Misfit has no
illusions about himself and responds to her desperate
flattery with the matter-of-fact answer: " 'Nome, I ain't
a good man' " (139). What is significant here, I think,
is that The Misfit, like Hazel Motes in *Wise Blood* and
Tarwater in *The Violent Bear It Away,* and unlike both
the positivists and the positive thinkers, takes the question of good and evil seriously. While his self-appropri-
ated name connects him, with superb irony, to the
world of popular psychology and textbook sociology in
which he is merely a deviant from society's norms, The
Misfit himself sees his problem religiously and meta-
physically. His final speech to the old lady sums up his
radical vision of man's state:

> "Jesus was the only One that ever raised the dead, . . .
> and He shouldn't have done it. He thown everything off
> balance. If He did what He said, then it's nothing for you
> to do but thow away everything and follow Him, and if

He didn't, then it's nothing for you to do but enjoy the few minutes you got left the best way you can—by killing somebody or burning down his house or doing some other meanness to him. No pleasure but meanness."
(P. 142)

A Southern "poor white" cousin of Dostoevsky's tortured agnostics, The Misfit decides that either Jesus told the truth about Himself, in which case one should stake his entire existence on Him, or else He was deluded, the logical inference of this being "God is dead." And since the latter seems to be the case, signifying that good is not the determinative principle of the universe, The Misfit concludes, much like the Dostoevskian hero, that "everything is permissible."

The point which this story decisively makes is that, while a good man is indeed hard to find, a truly evil one is just as rare. The Misfit, in his frustrated search for some assurance of the reality and permanence of good, turns to evil as a not-very-satisfactory but logical alternative to the wholly specious "good" offered him by contemporary society and exemplified in the selfish, self-indulgent, easy-conscienced grandmother. To society, The Misfit is a psychopathic killer: to Flannery O'Connor he would seem to be a kind of saint *manqué*, cutting through the cliché-ridden, heedless lives of the people he murders to radical questions of depth, of spirit, of the reality of good and evil as ontological entities. In his terrifyingly perverted lucidity, The Misfit implies that, if evil is defined as mere maladjustment, the concept of good then becomes meaningless. By insisting that he himself is *not* a good man, The Misfit evinces a rudimentary awareness of goodness as a possibility, even if not for him. Moreover, to be truly human, The Misfit seems to say, man must be committed to either good or evil and must *do* good or evil; and since there appears to be no sanction for goodness—

and such a sanction is precisely what The Misfit longs for and can not find—he must therefore commit himself to evil. The Misfit reminds us of Dostoevsky's conviction that "crime does not indicate any natural amorality" but is rather a negative testimony to a good, apart from which man can scarcely live [4]; and, in his final comment that there is no real pleasure in life, i.e., that even acts of evil provide no genuine fulfillment, this Christ-haunted criminal from the backwoods of Georgia intimates just how deep is his intuitive penetration into the mystery of good and evil which so tormented Dostoevsky.

The three stories just examined bear a certain family resemblance in that each presents the encounter— sometimes violent and always unnerving—of a self-righteous and "inauthentic" female character with a masculine embodiment of disruptive, irrational, even terrifying power from a world beyond the predictable, ordered existence of the female protagonist. Considered apart from the other stories in this collection, these three would lead one to conclude that Flannery O'Connor held to a "double standard" of sorts, by which women are judged as more prone to complacency and self-deception than are men. Stanley Hyman speaks of her female characters as being largely "self-intoxicated," [5] and there is sufficient evidence to warrant such a generalization. In the O'Connor world, however, self-intoxication is not a vice to which women have exclusive rights.

Flannery O'Connor's female exemplars of self-intoxication are often drawn with deftness and with an unerring sense of the *mot juste* necessary to expose their moral flaccidity and spiritual emptiness. But among her finest achievements in characterization must certainly be included those masters of hypocrisy, duplicity, and/or self-deception, the masculine spokesmen for morality and religion who are at bottom rascals and frauds—such figures as Hoover Shoats (*Wise Blood*), Manley Pointer ("Good Country People"), and Tom T. Shiftlet, the wandering, one-armed handy man of "The Life You Save May Be Your Own." Shiftlet is an especially interesting psychological type because to a large extent he himself is taken in by the pious cant which is his hallmark. Manley Pointer is a scoundrel and knows it; Pointer, in fact, revels in his knavery. Shiftlet is a victim of his own rhetoric. The person he cons most consistently is himself.

Another male character from this collection who is self-intoxicated is Mr. Head, the protagonist of "The Artificial Nigger," Miss O'Connor's own favorite among her stories. Seen from Mr. Head's initial point of view, the narrative's subject is a child's initiation into the adult world of good and evil. In fact, the story's true impact derives not so much from the fall of a child into the morally ambiguous world of adult experience, as from the fall of his guide from boastful claims of virtual omniscience to acknowledgment of ignorance and spiritual poverty.

Mr. Head awakens at two o'clock on the morning he is to take his grandson, Nelson, on his first visit to the city. Although Mr. Head has himself been there only twice, he pretends to knowledge of city life in order to maintain a tenuous supremacy over the excessively independent and self-willed boy. As the first paragraphs reveal, however, the grandson's inordinate faith in the sufficiency of his unaided intellect is a reflection of the old man's own self-pride. Lifting his head from the pillow, Mr. Head observes the moon flooding the room; then in a mirror he watches the moon hesitate, or so it seems to him, "as if it were waiting for his permission to enter." In the "miraculous moonlight" the floor appears silver and "the ticking on his pillow . . . brocade" (195). Wherever the moon reaches it spreads a "dignifying light," and in its transforming aura, Mr. Head's eyes have a "look of composure and of ancient wisdom as if they belonged to one of the great guides of men" (195). This is exactly how Mr. Head perceives himself: as a man of strong will and character, ripened by years and experience, imbued with "that calm understanding of life that makes [one] a suitable guide for the young" (195). The moonlight, whose magic distorts as it illumines, gives us Mr. Head as he would like to think of himself. Moreover, it establishes the religious-poetic context within which the old man's "initiation" is to be understood: "He might have been Vergil summoned in the middle of the night to go to Dante or better, Raphael, awakened by a blast of God's light to fly to the side of Tobias" (195). Significantly, only the spot where Nelson lies beneath the window is untouched by the moon's light, indicating the limits of the old man's self-glorifying vision.

The flattering view of Mr. Head which the moonlight affords is, of course, presented ironically, since in the day's events he is to be both guide and principal initiate, discovering through the agency of the boy (whom he insists on patronizing) the abysmal vanity of his pride and the overpowering force of God's mercy. The irony is magnified when we learn that Nelson, though only ten, manages so to plague his grandfather with dogmatic declarations of his knowledge and competence that the old man is genuinely threatened by the boy's assertiveness and must counterattack with the suggestion that, because of his limited experience, Nelson will quite likely not recognize a Negro when he sees one.

The grandfather's unreliability as a guide is foreshadowed in an event occurring prior to the journey. Having awakened an hour earlier than necessary, Mr. Head allows himself to fall asleep again certain that he will reawaken in ample time to prepare for the trip. When he rouses later to find his grandson already dressed and cooking breakfast, Mr. Head feels compelled to remind Nelson of his ignorance and on the train later he repeats his reminder, though this time in the presence of a stranger whom Mr. Head wishes to impress: " 'Ignorant as the day he was born, but I mean for him to get his fill once and for all' " (199). Mr. Head's declared intention, in undertaking his "moral mission," is to introduce Nelson to the "evil" city, which the old man can then claim to have encompassed in his infinite wisdom and dismissed as a mere " 'nigger heaven' " (206). In this way, he assures himself, he can return home with the boy's ego deflated.

Hence it is with the utmost consternation that Mr. Head views Nelson's enthusiastic response to the metropolis, and he moves swiftly to dampen his fervor by pointing out to him the city's "sinister" side—its system of sewers, "endless pitchblack tunnels" into which a person might be sucked without warning. In the frame of reference established by the earlier comparison of Mr. Head and Vergil, the bowels of the city immediately call to mind Dante's Inferno. It is Nelson himself who "connect[s] the sewer passages with the entrance to hell," and who, with considerable fright, considers how a person might indeed become lost forever should he fall into one of the entrances. His alarm is momentary, however, for he soon asserts that " 'you can stay away from the holes,' " a declaration of self-confidence which leaves Mr. Head "dismayed." As Nelson had predicted, the two of them become lost, and Mr. Head must suffer the humiliation of his grandson's accusations as the boy mutters from time to time, " 'First you lost the sack [containing their lunch] and then you lost the way' " (206). When at last they stop to rest and Nelson dozes briefly, Mr. Head, determined to teach the boy a lesson, conceals himself around a nearby corner. Nelson wakes with a start, and bolts down the street with such speed that the old man loses him momentarily. When he does finally locate the boy, he comes upon a scene that fills him with dread. On the street lies a woman, shouting that her ankle is broken and that " 'your daddy'll pay for it! Every nickel! Police! Police!' " (209) Nelson rushes to his grandfather, desperately flinging his arms about his hips. The scene—which constitutes the turning point of the story —deserves extended quotation:

> Mr. Head was trying to detach Nelson's fingers from the flesh in the back of his legs. The old man's head lowered itself into his collar like a turtle's; his eyes were glazed with fear and caution.
>
> "Your boy has broken my ankle!" the old woman shouted. "Police!"
>
> Mr. Head sensed the approach of the policeman from behind. He stared straight ahead at the women who were massed in their fury like a solid wall to block his escape. "This is not my boy," he said. "I never seen him before."
>
> *He felt Nelson's fingers fall out of his flesh.*
>
> The women dropped back, staring at him with horror, as if they were so repulsed by a man who would deny his own image and likeness that they could not bear to lay hands on him. Mr. Head walked on, through a space they silently cleared, and left Nelson behind. Ahead of him he saw nothing but a hollow tunnel that had once been the street [emphasis added]. (Pp. 209–10)

Mr. Head's denial has been compared to the denial of Christ by Judas and Peter [6] but clearly involved also is a denial of part of Mr. Head himself. Not only is Nelson flesh of his flesh (as the emphasized line in the quoted passage implies) and also his "image and likeness"; he is—and this is more essential—a living embodiment of Mr. Head's intellectual pride and moral boast-

ing. Hence the old man's denial of the boy is tantamount to the death of that aspect of himself which
Nelson represents. As his former, presumably self-sufficient ego perishes in the harsh glare of daylight, carrying
with it the "dignified" self-image of lunar magic, Mr.
Head begins to experience the reality of damnation. The
Dantesque overtones of this experience are evoked when
he encounters suburban drives which wind "around and
around in endless ridiculous circles" (211). Mr. Head's
feeling of perdition becomes so intense that he imagines
himself being sucked, willingly, into one of the sewer
entrances.

With Nelson's eyes penetrating his back "like pitch-
fork prongs," Mr. Head attempts to heal the broken
relationship by offering to buy a Coca Cola (an obvious
simulation of the communion rite), but Nelson responds with a reproachful stare. Overwhelmed by anguish, the old man cries out: " 'I'm lost!' . . . 'I'm lost
and can't find my way and me and this boy have got to
catch this train and I can't find the station. Oh Gawd
I'm lost. Oh hep me Gawd I'm lost!' " (211).

Given directions to the station by a passing stranger,
Mr. Head feels momentary relief, but is again frozen by
Nelson's unforgiving, "triumphantly cold" eyes, which
intensify his despair. Suddenly, as if providentially
timed, Mr. Head and Nelson undergo an experience
deeply imbued with mystical overtones; and it is out of
this common experience that Mr. Head receives the real
answer to his prayer. On the edge of a lawn before them,
Mr. Head spies a battered plaster statue of a Negro.
The old man is rendered momentarily speechless before
this wholly unfamiliar and unexpected phenomenon and
then exclaims in an awed tone, " 'An artifical nigger.' "
His words are repeated by Nelson with precisely the
same intonation and at this moment the old man and
his other self, his "likeness and image," seem to blend

and to be united again in the mutuality of their apprehension of a mystifying OTHER.

> The two of them stood there with their necks forward at almost the same angle and their shoulders curved in almost exactly the same way and their hands trembling identically in their pockets. *Mr. Head looked like an ancient child and Nelson like a miniature old man.* They stood gazing at the artificial Negro as if they were faced with some great mystery, some monument to another's victory that brought them together in their common defeat. They could both feel it dissolving their differences like an action of mercy. Mr. Head had never known before what mercy felt like because he had been too good to deserve any, but he felt he knew now [emphasis added]. (Pp. 212–13)

So profound is this shared moment of grace that Mr. Head and Nelson appear to exchange places with one another, the isolated and alienated ego of each joining itself to that of the other as they undergo what is a virtual death and rebirth of the self.

The reconciliation is wrought out of a strange and (to them) inexplicable fact of reality, marking the completion of Mr. Head's initiation. The disparity between his former exalted image of himself and the actual frail and fallible human reality is too glaring to be any longer denied. Nelson, too, has been chastened (" 'I'm glad I've went once, but I'll never go back again!' " [214]), but appropriately it is the older man who has learned most from the journey. As they alight from the train in the clearing near their home, the moonlight again floods the scene. But this time the imagery suggests not a nobleman's castle but rather a garden whose denizens are beholden to divine providence for their happiness and safety: "The treetops, fencing the junction like the protecting walls of a garden, were darker than the sky which was hung with gigantic white clouds illuminated like lanterns" (213). Mr. Head's fall has indeed led to expulsion from Eden, or, more accurately, from a falsely secure garden-world whose terraces are built upon the specious sufficiency of the self; his restoration, both the imagery and authorial comment insist, is to the true garden of salvation, watered by the ever-flowing rivers of God's mercy.

> Mr. Head stood very still and felt the action of mercy touch him again but this time he knew that there were no words in the world that could name it. He understood that it grew out of agony, . . . He stood appalled, judging himself with the thoroughness of God, while the action of mercy covered his pride like a flame and consumed it. (P. 213)

Here, in the penultimate paragraph, Miss O'Connor permits herself an explicitness of theological statement which is rarely found in her work. That she is able to do so, without marring the dramatic effectiveness of the story, is accounted for principally by an exquisitely delicate balance of imagery and symbolic reference, action and authorial comment, which the narrative as a whole achieves. The authorial comment, especially at the end, might have made the didactic element ponderous had the artistic achievement been less impressive.

Several of Miss O'Connor's principal devices—the elaborate moon symbolism, the recurring Dantean motif, the complex psychological relationship of Mr. Head and Nelson—have already been examined. Another element, crucial to the story's dramatic and moral impact, is the symbolic role of the NEGRO. It will be recalled that Mr. Head uses the fact that Nelson has never seen a Negro as a ploy in his struggle to maintain dominance over his grandson. So often is this fact repeated that the Negro comes to stand for Nelson's general ignorance of the world. Hence, it is appropriate that the crucial scene on the train should involve the passing down the aisle of "a huge coffee-colored man" whom Nelson, who had been confident that he would "know a nigger if [he saw] one," is unable to identify. Not only is the man immense, but he has about him an opulent and majestic air, and, since he fails to correspond to the stereotype of the Negro which Nelson has acquired from his grandfather, he represents more than a mere sign of *Nelson's* ignorance. He is a symbol of that which is beyond the ordinary, that which transcends man's expectations and eludes his calculations, in brief, that which is mysterious. And it is the incalculable and mysterious which both Nelson and Mr. Head fear, since it calls into question their greatest treasure—their supposed omniscience.

Later, as Mr. Head and the boy wander through the Negro section of the city, lost and increasingly aware of their helplessness, Nelson approaches another large Negro, this time a woman. The woman is described in such a fashion as to evoke all of her sensuous feminine qualities, and Nelson is as attracted to her as he was repelled by the man on the train. In each case, however, there is a character of mystery about the encounter, and on this occasion the mystery threatens to engulf him. As he asks for directions, Nelson feels "his breath drawn up by the woman's dark eyes" (206). "He stood drinking in every detail of her. . . . He suddenly wanted her to reach down and pick him up and draw him against her and then he wanted to feel her breath on his face. He wanted to look down and down into her eyes while she held him tighter and tighter. He had never had such a feeling before. He felt as if he were reeling down through a pitchblack tunnel" (206–7). Remarkable for its erotic detail, this passage seems to demand a Freudian interpretation. At the very least it must be admitted that the woman with her "bare arm" and "tremendous bosom" appears to represent a sexual object which awakens latent erotic sensations in Nelson. Moreover, as we have been told earlier that the boy's mother died while he was still a baby and that he has never known any other women, we may safely conclude that this woman—so earthy, so substantial, so self-possessed—assumes for him the character of a mother figure. The final sentence, with the explicitly sexual overtones of the image of the "pitchblack tunnel," suggests the complexity and ambiguity of the boy's reaction and reveals Nelson's unconscious desire to be absorbed into the protecting mother.

What is perhaps most significant, however, about Nelson's response to the Negro woman is the sense of wonder evoked in him by that which is fundamentally different, that which by its strangeness and compelling "thereness"—in this case, WOMAN, MOTHER, NEGRO—shatters his narrow, self-contained view of reality. This experience, together with the morning's events on the train, provides the basis for Nelson's response to the "artificial nigger." Since all of his expectations concerning Negroes have been frustrated by contact with real ones, the discovery that there are also "artificial" ones implies a world far more mysterious than he had dreamt possible. In the face of this final mystery, both Nelson and Mr. Head are confounded and made equal by this "monument to another's victory," and, as equalizer, the statue becomes a medium of grace. The marvelous appropriateness of this—that the Negro, a traditional symbol in the American South of inequality among men, should be the agent of effecting an acknowledgment of essential human equality—can scarcely be exaggerated. And that it should be a chipped plaster figure, with "a wild look of misery," which serves as the agent of human reconciliation and as a sign of the magnitude of God's mercy is appropriate

also. For this "crucified" Negro, made of clay and
grotesque in the contrast of its intended expression of
happiness and its actual look of affliction, constitutes an
analogue of the Christian belief that the lowly, the
despised, the insignificant ("the least of these") may
well be the chosen means of divine revelation.[7]

In her essays and lectures, Flannery O'Connor frequently expressed the conviction that mystery can only
be adumbrated through the mundane, the natural, the
"what-is." Elaborating upon this idea while addressing
an audience at the College of St. Teresa in Minnesota,
she remarked: "the Christian novelist lives in a larger
universe [than does the naturalistic writer]. He believes
that the natural world contains the supernatural. And
this doesn't mean that his obligation to portray the
natural is less; it means it is greater." [8] It is this "en-
larged" universe to which Flannery O'Connor sought to
give body. In "The Artificial Nigger," it seems to me,
she realized this purpose in a degree seldom matched in
her early fiction.

Driskell and Brittain make an elaborate case for the
thematic unity of this volume, contending that the
stories are arranged in a progression which moves from
the fall of man, symbolized by the Tower of Babel (in
the title story a key conversation regarding the scarcity
of good men takes place in a diner called The Tower),
to the vicarious atonement and promise of salvation
embodied in the one good man of the collection, Mr.
Guizac, the "displaced person" of the final story.[9] Another kind of thematic unity may be deduced from the
prominent role in this collection of questions which are
an outgrowth of the grandmother's encounter with The
Misfit: What are the constitutive elements of good and
evil, how are they incarnated in human attitudes and
behavior, and, given the moral and metaphysical confusion of the modern world, how can one be certain

that what seems to be good is truly good and that what seems to be evil is truly evil?

Most of the stories in *A Good Man Is Hard to Find* point to deception and self-deception as the chief sources of evil. And the most destructive consequence of both is alienation—alienation from one's self, from others, and from the source of one's being, God. These themes, it need hardly be said, are at least as old as the Book of Genesis. Equally as old is the theme of idolatry, which, in the biblical context, is viewed as the ultimate consequence of self-deception and alienation. Man *must* worship, so both the biblical authors and Flannery O'Connor appear to believe, and when he no longer worships the true God, he makes for himself false ones.

Thus Hulga, described as "someone who has achieved blindness by an act of the will and means to keep it" (244), is the prototype of the self-deceiver. As her blindness is near-total, so is her alienation. Her idols, as we have seen, are cold rationality, self-sufficiency involving contempt for others, and, more deeply embedded in her consciousness, a utopian dream of evading the results of the fall through a return to innocence by way of a purely human love in which there is none of the cost of love manifest in the crucifixion. As her various idols are smashed Hulga experiences a crucifixion of the old self. Whether the experience will lead to recognition of the true nature of the self and its dependence upon a Power beyond itself is a question which the story does not answer. As is typical of Miss O'Connor's art, the action of "Good Country People" brings the reader face to face with both the mystery of human personality and a mystery yet more ultimate.

Flannery O'Connor once put the matter thus: "The artist penetrates the concrete world in order to find at its depths the image of its source, the image of ultimate reality. This in no way hinders his perception of evil but rather sharpens it." [10] I would add that it in no way hinders his perception of good either, but it makes very difficult the recognition of good since any superficial embodiment is excluded. The Misfit's comment, made in reference to the grandmother, that "She would of been a good woman . . . if it had been somebody there to shoot her every minute of her life" provides a clue to Flannery O'Connor's understanding of the nature of good. On this point it seems to me that Flannery O'Connor's view does not differ greatly from that of certain Christian existentialists. Good, for man living under the dispensation of the fall, is constant awareness of one's finitude and of the nearness of death; it is living each moment with absolute fidelity to that truth and with resolute honesty in accepting one's fears and anxieties and acknowledging one's frailties; it is, above all, living without illusions, recognizing the vulnerability of the self but also recognizing a transcendent Power which sustains the self even in its moments of greatest anxiety and deepest despair. Thus, while Mr. Guizac is clearly the person most fully associated with Christ and Christ's sacrifice (Mrs. McIntyre's comment that "Christ was just another D.P." is only one of many clues to that identification), I think the most convincing good man of this collection may be Mr. Head, whose movement from proud self-sufficiency to despair to forgiveness and grace is more fully dramatized than that of any other character in the entire O'Connor corpus.

4

The Violent Bear It Away

Flannery O'Connor's second novel, *The Violent Bear
It Away* (1960), was a long time in the making. Writing
to Robert Fitzgerald in 1953 she reported on a novel
which appeared "to be doing very well" and commented
that one of its characters was a "nice gangster" named
Rufus Florida Johnson.[1] This character and presumably
the entire novel underwent a complete metamorphosis,
since Francis Marion Tarwater, who is the published
work's protagonist and obvious successor to Rufus
Johnson, possesses what might be described as criminal
inclinations but can scarcely be called a gangster. Rufus
Johnson, more compulsive in his criminality than is
Tarwater, suffered his own change of fortunes, becoming
the delinquent with the clubfoot and the high I.Q. who
proves to the social worker Sheppard, in the story of
that title, that indeed "The Lame Shall Enter First."
Tarwater, however, is a type of the criminal-compulsive
in that he, like Hazel Motes and The Misfit, is caught
on the horns of the faith-doubt dilemma and is able to
free himself only through commission of an act which
constitutes, in a sense even more paradoxical than usual,
"spiritual crime."

The novel's epigraph, from St. Matthew's Gospel,
reads as follows: "From the days of John the Baptist
until now, the kingdom of heaven suffereth violence,

and the violent bear it away." Both the title and the passage from which it is taken are enigmatic, and a good deal of controversy has arisen concerning Miss O'Connor's intention in the novel as implied in the epigraph. Having examined both the translation of the Authorized Version and that of the New English Bible, Stanley Hyman concludes that the meaning of the quotation is "that the violent are enemies of the kingdom, capturing it from the righteous." [2] This interpretation might have validity if there were in the novel any nonviolent righteous from whom the kingdom might be captured; but this is not the case. The only righteous persons discovered here are old Mason Tarwater and his great-nephew Francis Tarwater and they are indeed violent, though not, I think, totally insane as a number of critics, including Hyman, would have us believe.

In this novel Miss O'Connor dealt more directly than in any of her other fictions with the theme of prophetism. That the vocation of the prophet was one of her abiding concerns we know from Sr. Kathleen Feeley's careful documentation of Flannery O'Connor's markings, annotations, and notes in her books on the Old Testament. That she believed the artist to share in this vocation we know from her nonfictional writings. Time and again we encounter in *Mystery and Manners* reference to the fiction writer as prophet. The following excerpt is especially revelatory, for it sheds light upon both the theological and the aesthetic presuppositions which underlie this author's practice:

> The fiction writer should be characterized by his kind of vision. His kind of vision is prophetic vision. Prophecy, which is dependent on the imaginative and not the moral faculty, need not be a matter of predicting the future. The prophet is a realist of distances. . . . It is [this kind of] realism which does not hesitate to distort appearances in order to show a hidden truth.[3]

Here Miss O'Connor reiterates her conviction, touched upon in Chapter I, that in practicing his art with integrity, the fiction writer projects his vision beyond the surfaces of reality to a deeper reality or "hidden truth." That this effort often involves distortion is an inevitable consequence of the prophet-artist's calling to penetrate the depth of "what-is," to be a "seer." Both Flannery O'Connor as artist and the prophets she creates in this novel are distorters; but the distorters, she would argue, are, like Hazel Motes in his blaspheming, truer than those whose standard is a lukewarm normality.

Almost everyone who has written on this novel has focused upon this most obvious motif of the prophet's calling. Stuart L. Burns in his *Sewanee Review* piece, "Flannery O'Connor's *The Violent Bear It Away*: Apotheosis in Failure," brings to his reading of the novel a sensitive awareness of the ambiguities inherent in the situation involving the apparently self-appointed prophet, old Mason Tarwater, and his unwilling disciple, young Tarwater. Stanley Hyman too concentrates largely upon the theme of prophetism and, in fact, states without qualification that the novel is "wholly and centrally about Vocation and the prophet's necessary stage of resistance to Vocation." [4] Mr. Hyman likens the struggle of the fourteen-year-old protagonist to avoid his calling to that of Moses and Jonah and proposes that, in Tarwater's final acceptance of his burden to be "both vessel and instrument of divine purpose," there is to be found the story's deepest meaning: "Divine purpose is not answerable to human reason." [5] As far as it goes, this interpretation is certainly defensible: Tarwater *is* a reluctant prophet, he does in time come to feel that it is his inexorable destiny to trudge "into the distance in the bleeding stinking mad shadow of Jesus," [6] and his ultimate realization that there is no escaping this fate does suggest that divine purpose will have its way with man, even though man's reason or his will would have it otherwise. But Hyman's reading of the novel seems to me inadequate, for it might just as plausibly be argued that, rather than being "wholly and centrally about Vocation," the novel concerns itself in large part with the difference between two ways of interpreting reality, and that the story of Tarwater's efforts to flee the call of the Lord provides the necessary fictional context within which this difference may be examined and defined.

More specifically, I would submit that there are in the novel two more or less parallel lines of action which occasionally touch each other and which do at last decisively intersect, in one of the two major climaxes of the story—the baptismal drowning of the idiot child Bishop late in Chapter 9. There is, on the one hand, the struggle which takes place within Tarwater to throw off the influence of his great-uncle Mason Tarwater, a wild-eyed, half-mad backwoods prophet, who had kidnapped the boy when he was a baby and had raised him up to be, like himself, a prophet of the Lord. In this effort Tarwater is aided by a friendly "stranger," who appears in various disguises, real and fancied, and who is actually both Tarwater's alter ego and the devil. The stranger taunts Tarwater with the observation that true prophets receive from the Lord an unmistakable sign of their election and mutters sarcastically: "Lemme hear you prophesy something. The truth is the Lord ain't studying about you. You ain't entered His head" (325). Then, by way of further dissuading Tarwater from taking up his vocation, the stranger must discredit the boy's great-uncle, whom he accuses of having been crazy, or practically so, since he was a "one-notion man" who, year in and year out, talked of nothing but Jesus and salvation: "Ain't you in all your fourteen years of supporting his foolishness fed up and sick to the roof of your mouth with Jesus? My Lord and Saviour, the

stranger sighed, I am if you ain't" (326). In the voice of
the stranger one can hear that latent skepticism and
cynicism, that egocentric appeal to moderation and
common sense with which, it seems, every truly dedicated prophet must at one time or another struggle.
When Tarwater suggests that the choice he must make
is between Jesus and the devil, the stranger's prompt
reply is that, rather, the choice is between Jesus and self:
"No no no, the stranger said, there ain't no such thing
as a devil. I can tell you that from my own self-expe-
rience. . . . It ain't Jesus or the devil. It's Jesus or *you*"
(326).

There is another distinctly different, but related voice
in the novel, that of Tarwater's uncle, the schoolteacher
Rayber, who also attempts to persuade the boy that to
accept the mission bequeathed him by his great-uncle
is the sheerest madness. Here, in the confrontation between the fiercely independent, "primitive," uncouth
boy and the superficially educated and stubbornly determined rationalist Rayber, we may discern a fundamental clash between two radically opposed modes of
sensibility, between two different views of the world;
and the collision between the two makes for a second
line of action. Of course, the two struggles are insep-
arable parts of the one unified dramatic movement, but
it is essential in reading this work to keep clearly in
mind that Rayber represents not merely an added exacer-
bation of Tarwater's internal conflict but that in his
own right he stands for an understanding of human
existence which clashes violently with that of the old
prophet and which is finally judged, found wanting, and
rejected by Tarwater himself.

The son of old Mason Tarwater's sister and an insurance salesman who replied to his brother-in-law's
questions regarding the salvation of his soul with the
mocking assertion that he sold policies against all con-

tingencies, Rayber is himself haunted by childhood
memories of a pastoral paradise where he first learned
that his life counted because of the love of a Saviour.
Having been reared by parents who taught him nothing
more than not to wet the bed (so the old prophet tells
Tarwater), Rayber had come, when a lad of seven, to
old Tarwater's place Powderhead, there listening to the
old man talk of his redemption and then submitting to
baptism. The impression left by this experience is so
indelible that Rayber can never entirely shake off the
prophet's influence, though in time he comes to believe
that his uncle's religious fanaticism has done more to
scar his life than to save it. Years later, as the two confront each other over the baby Francis Marion Tarwater, the illegitimate son of Rayber's sister and grand-
nephew to the old man, Rayber accuses his uncle of
pushing him " 'out of the real world' " by filling him
with such " 'idiot hopes' " that at last he " 'didn't know
which was which' " (346). At this point the battle for
the soul of the baby is joined, as Rayber tells his uncle
that he will not permit him to " 'ruin another child's
life. This one is going to be brought up to live in the real
world,' " he declares. " '*He's going to be his own savior.
He's going to be free!*' " [emphasis added] (345). The
old man's determination is more than Rayber has
counted on, however, and at the first opportunity he
baptizes the baby (Rayber, to prove how free of superstition he is, proceeds to turn the child over and irrever-
ently pours water on his bottom) and, shortly after-
wards, kidnaps the child and returns to Powderhead
with him. Rayber's one attempt to retrieve the child
results in ignominious defeat when a blast from the old
prophet's shotgun carries away part of one ear, leaving
him permanently disfigured and partially deaf.

Fearing for his own sanity, Rayber imposes upon himself the strictest kind of discipline, countering the old

man's religious fanaticism with an emotional asceticism and a rationalistic fanaticism of his own, by means of which he hopes to control the irrational side of his nature. ("'What we understand we can control'" [417], he tells Tarwater.) But what Rayber cannot understand and can control only with the greatest difficulty is an impulse which is, to him, "completely irrational and abnormal": "a morbid surge of love that terrified him—powerful enough to throw him to the ground in an act of idiot praise" (372). Significantly, this "morbid surge of love" is particularly associated with Rayber's mentally defective child, Bishop, and would seem to connote (as the image of being thrown to the ground in praise suggests) a kind of mystical enthrallment with creation, including even its deformities (Bishop). Equally significant is the association in Rayber's mind of this overwhelming love with the old prophet: "It began with Bishop and then like an avalanche *covered everything his reason hated*. He always felt with it a rush of longing to have the old man's eyes—insane, fish-coloured, violent with their impossible vision of a world transfigured—turned on him once again. The longing was like an undertow in his blood dragging him backwards to what he knew to be madness" [emphasis added] (372). Good positivist that he is, Rayber understands love clinically and therapeutically and, as such, considers it to be valuable and useful. What frightens him is a love that man can not manipulate or control, can not put to use for his own or someone else's "improvement." It is the mystery of a love which seems to transcend human need and initiation that Rayber abhors—"love without reason . . . love that appeared to exist only to be itself, imperious and all demanding" (372).

As the novel opens, Tarwater, now fourteen, is preparing a grave for the body of his great-uncle who has just died. Instead of completing his task, however, he goes off to his uncle's still, gets thoroughly drunk and returns to the cabin after dark, setting fire to the structure as a kind of declaration of independence from the old man and as a final act of defiance of the father figure toward whom he has long felt both love and resentment. Much of his antagonism grows out of Tarwater's suspicion that his great-uncle may, after all, have been crazy and that in bringing him to this wild spot with only himself for tutor, the old man may have robbed him of valuable knowledge of the real world and of fourteen years of life in the city. Then, too, there is the old man's constant reference to Tarwater's freedom as "the freedom of the Lord Jesus Christ," and the boy, by nature extremely independent, finds the suggestion that his freedom is not self-generated a source of nagging irritation. However, the old prophet's years of labor have not been wasted, for no matter how ambivalent young Tarwater may be toward his great-uncle's command that he accomplish a task which the old man left unfinished (the baptizing of the idiot child Bishop), the boy's unwavering response to his uncle Rayber, to whose home he flees after the episode just described, is one of smouldering antipathy. Having for years heard the old man tell of how Rayber had once written an article about him, declaring him a "type that was almost extinct," and of how, when he realized that it was he, Mason Tarwater, to whom his nephew was referring, the old man "felt he was tied hand and foot inside the schoolteacher's head, a space as bare and neat as the cell in the asylum, and was shrinking, drying up to fit it" (348) — remembering all this the boy approaches his uncle with a mixture of wonder and dread. For the old man's warning that, with Rayber, his very selfhood would be in jeopardy has been too often repeated to be ignored: " 'And if you were to go there, the first thing

he would do would be to test your head and tell you
what you were thinking and how come you were thinking it and what you ought to be thinking instead. And
before long you wouldn't belong to your self no more,
you would belong to him' " (337).

The old man's prediction proves disturbingly accurate, for Tarwater finds, upon entering his uncle's
house, that he is scrutinized by "two small drill-like
eyes," seemingly intent upon boring to the very depths
of his soul (355). Instinctively, young Tarwater draws
away from this creature who strikes him as being a kind
of mechanical man, with his "black-rimmed glasses"
and his electrical hearing aid—a device increasingly referred to in the novel as "the machine." After an exchange in which Tarwater, bent on asserting his independence from the start, facetiously asks the teacher if
his " 'head light[s] up,' " Rayber begins to try to win the
boy's confidence and to free him from what he considers the bondage of "false guilt" and ignorance in
which the old prophet had left him. Rayber himself
suffers feelings of guilt for not having made a greater
effort to save Tarwater, while still a baby, from the
warping influence of the old man; and frustrated in his
efforts to apply his advanced educational theories to
his idiot son, he sees in his young nephew a chance both
to redeem the past and to shape a human life after a
pattern of his own design. In his arrogant assurance that
he can at last best the old man by undoing the work of
fourteen years, Rayber tries to establish an intimate
relationship with the boy, calling him Frankie and assuring him that he at last has a friend. " 'You have more
than a friend now,' " he declares; " 'you have a father.' "
Tarwater's reply—immediate, scornful, defiant—marks
him as irredeemably the child of the old prophet:
" 'I ain't ast for no father,' " he twice repeats. " 'I'm out
of the womb of a whore. . . . And my name ain't
Frankie' " (368).

From this point forward, while Tarwater fights his inner battle to resolve the conflict between that part of himself which is repelled by the call to prophecy and that part which cannot deny the old man's commission, another battle takes place in which Tarwater's will is pitted against Rayber's (the second line of action). And here, I think, we come closer to the heart of Flannery O'Connor's vision. For what is most centrally involved in *this* struggle are two radically divergent concepts of freedom. As we have already seen, old Tarwater had believed that in Rayber the power of mind, of the Idea, was grown so rampant as made it inevitable that he should entrap and shrink to nothingness the selfhood of anyone on whom he might chance to fasten. Rayber is, in fact, presented as a kind of monster of abstract intellect, capable of peering "through the actual *insignificant* boy . . . to an image of him that he held fully developed in his mind" [emphasis added] (357). And young Tarwater is determined that no one, and especially not his uncle, shall rob him of his freedom. Thus, when Rayber attempts to give the boy an intelligence test, Tarwater remembers the old man's warning and hisses at the schoolteacher: " 'I'm free. I'm outside your head. I ain't in it. I ain't in it and I ain't about to be' " (371). The schoolteacher, certain that the boy is a victim of a compulsive neurosis, a consequence of years spent with the old prophet, responds predictably: " 'You don't know what freedom is' " (371). To Rayber the boy's every action exhibits an independence which could only have been acquired from the old man—"not a constructive independence but one that was irrational, backwoods, and ignorant" (365).

Yet, for all his talk of freedom and constructive independence, Rayber himself is anything but free. Thinking of himself as an emancipated modern man, totally divested of religious belief, and capable, through the most rigorous application of will power, of controlling what seems to him an irrational psychic undertow, Rayber is, in fact, a victim of his own intellectual habits which cause him to substitute thought for life. This was the old man's most perceptive observation regarding his nephew, that he lives, as Rayber himself admits, with his "guts in [his] head," and that this condition renders him incapable of acting: " 'It was me could act,' " the prophet says, " 'not him. . . . He could only get everything inside his head and grind it to nothing' " (349). And so, when, late in the novel, Rayber resolves to confront Tarwater with his analysis of the boy's difficulty and announces that, while they are both plagued by compulsive tendencies, he (Rayber) at least has no compulsion to baptize Bishop, we can hear the old man's voice, distinct and filled with contempt, in Tarwater's retort: " 'It ain't the same. . . . I can pull it up by the roots, once and for all. I can do something. I ain't like you. All you can do is think what you would have done if you had done it. Not me. I can do it. I can act. . . . It's nothing about me like you' " (418).

When Tarwater does finally decide to act, his prophecy is fulfilled: he acts decisively, drowning the idiot boy in a lake where the three of them have gone for an outing, while Rayber, who had himself once attempted to drown the child and had discovered that he was incapable of the deed, lies in bed, silently acquiescing in the death of his son. Moments before, he had been struck with the realization that all he desires is for the world to be consumed, and at the thought of his own destruction he feels utter indifference. Discovering at last his true self, Rayber wishes only to be a passive "observer" of the final holocaust, thinking that "this indifference was the most that human dignity could achieve. . . . To feel nothing was peace" (421). The absolute desolation of Rayber's soul could hardly be more graphically portrayed than in Flannery O'Connor's final description of him as he stands at the window overlooking the lake, his heart beating with a "dull mechanical beat": "He stood waiting for the raging pain, the intolerable hurt that was his due, to begin, so that he could ignore it, but he continued to feel nothing. He stood light-headed at the window and it was not until he realized there would be no pain that he collapsed" (423). Rayber's ruthless control of his emotions brings him at last that freedom from the irrational undertow for which he has so long striven; but, to his dismay, he discovers that to feel nothing is not peace but horror. Having trod for years the razor's edge between madness and emptiness, he finds at last that the old man (through Tarwater) has beaten him again—not by plunging him into a frenzy of "idiot praise" but by constantly presenting him with an option which, in his steadfast refusal, leaves him finally alone in an utter void. Rayber achieves his freedom—freedom from Bishop whom he looks upon as a mere mistake of nature; freedom from Tarwater, whom he has gradually come to hate; and freedom from the "morbid surge of love" which, terrifyingly, has long lurked in his dark subconsciousness. But the price he must pay for this freedom is high indeed, for in achieving it he sacrifices an essential part of his humanity.

And what of Tarwater's freedom? If he remains outside the schoolteacher's head, is he not still a victim of the old man's monomania? For, when he drowns Bishop as an ostensible act of defiance and a final repudiation of his calling (with the stranger, now his "faithful friend," standing alongside, urging him to the deed), Tarwater utters involuntarily the words of baptism. Of course, he explains to himself that this was simply an accident and that his drowning the child far outweighs his baptizing him. Confident that his act does constitute an irrevocable "No!" Tarwater starts out for Powder-

head, thinking that it was not as a boy "that he returned. He returned tried in the fire of his refusal, with
all the old man's fancies burnt out of him, with all the
old man's madness smothered for good, so that there
was never any chance it would break out in him. He had
saved himself forever" (434). But before reaching his
destination he accepts a ride with a stranger whom we
recognize as Tarwater's faithful friend the devil, now in
the guise of a city slicker homosexual. The stranger
drugs Tarwater and rapes him, and, when the boy
awakens, he is so repelled by the incident that he sets
fire to the bushes about him, in an effort to burn clean
the "evil ground" wherever touched by the stranger.
Tarwater moves forward to Powderhead, no longer believing that there he will live out his refusal but rather
knowing that it is his fate to discover there a "final
revelation." His eyes, the reader is told, "looked as if,
touched with a coal like the lips of the prophet, they
would never be used for ordinary sights again" (442).

The rest, one might say, is epilogue. Tarwater returns
to Powderhead, where he finds his great-uncle's grave
marked by a rude cross (the old man had been dragged
from the shack by a local Negro and given a Christian
burial while the boy was off getting drunk). And, here,
he is indeed granted an ultimate revelation. On the
entire journey from the lake to Powderhead, Tarwater
has been beset by a raging thirst and an insatiable hunger, and as the boy reaches what was once his home, he
feels the hunger attack him with renewed force. Standing motionless before the piercing, judging eyes of the
Negro Buford, and recognizing in the grave with its
cross a sign of the faith he has, unconsciously, held all
his life, Tarwater undergoes a transforming mystical
experience—that "final revelation" in which he sees a
multitude, among whom is the old man, being fed from
a "single basket." The old prophet seems to lean for-

ward and the boy repeats his motion, "aware at last of
the object of his hunger, aware that it was the same as
the old man's and that nothing on earth would fill him"
(446). Turning toward the encircling forest, Tarwater
sees "a red-gold tree of fire ascend[ing] as if it would
consume the darkness in one tremendous burst of flame"
(447). Knowing that at last he has received his sign, his
own burning bush, Tarwater throws himself upon the
grave of the old prophet and hears the long-awaited
command: GO WARN THE CHILDREN OF GOD
OF THE TERRIBLE SPEED OF MERCY.

It can be argued, of course, that Tarwater is simply
what Rayber takes him to be—a victim of a neurotic
compulsion by which he is finally overborne. In this interpretation, Tarwater's freedom is no more a reality
than is Rayber's. But, in the economy of the story itself,
it is evident that Tarwater, as he so often boasts, makes
things happen and is empowered to act. Furthermore, I
think it safe to assume that it was Flannery O'Connor's conviction that, to be genuine, freedom must be
grounded in commitment of some sort and must have a
definite object, otherwise it becomes what Francis Fergusson in his discussion of Ibsen's *Ghosts* characterized
as "the anomalous 'freedom' of undefined and unin-
formed aspiration"—*Unendlichkeit*.[7] Naturally, that
commitment need not be a Christian commitment, but
it is clear that Flannery O'Connor took a very skeptical
view of what is achievable in the way of freedom, on the
basis of a secularist ordering of human life.

Her manner of stating the problem in her fiction,
however, has led some critics to accuse her of denying
altogether the possibility of human freedom. One reviewer of *The Violent Bear It Away*, himself a Roman
Catholic novelist, alleged that the novel was thoroughly
"anti-Catholic," since it constituted a systematic refuta-
tion of such central Catholic dogma as the justice of

God and the freedom of mankind to choose or reject redemption.[8] The thesis of this reviewer is not likely to persuade the unprejudiced reader, but others, reading the same novel, have made similar charges and with a good deal more cogency. One of these finds in Miss O'Connor's fiction an allegorical rendering of the human situation in which it is the destiny of all men to be faced with the choice of God or a deforming and self-destructive godlessness.[9] Flannery O'Connor, so Thomas Lorch maintains, imposes upon her characters the a priori assumption that man is innately religious, and it is this assumption which causes her to offer the characters in her work only two choices: submission to an all-demanding God or immersion in soul-rotting evil. But such a severe limitation upon choice appears to preclude genuine, existential freedom. Even when Flannery O'Connor attempted to resolve the question, Lorch avers, she succeeded verbally perhaps but not actually. Her most forthright statement on the subject is contained in the brief prefatory note to the 1962 edition of *Wise Blood*. There she says, "Does one's integrity ever lie in what he is not able to do? I think that usually it does, for free will does not mean one will, but many wills conflicting in one man. Freedom cannot be conceived simply. It is a mystery and one which a novel . . . can only be asked to deepen." [10] This formulation Lorch finds unconvincing, for in practice Miss O'Connor's characters must pay a terrible price for their choice of God, it being nothing less than their individual selves, their own peculiar identities. Tarwater, for instance, "must choose between becoming himself and becoming, in effect, his great-uncle." [11] Throughout both *Wise Blood* and *The Violent* the demands of commitment to God require a relinquishment of self tantamount, in Lorch's opinion, to destruction of the personality. The ultimate implication of Miss O'Connor's fictional treatment of freedom appears then to be that man, relent-lessly pursued by the Hound of Heaven, has no meaning-ful choice, since what purports to be free choice is really decision for a God who commands violent self-abnega-tion and madness or for the nothingness of evil and self-destruction.

Granting that there is a high degree of complexity in Flannery O'Connor's treatment of the problem of faith and freedom, I think it should be pointed out that no-where does she suggest that all men either do or should possess that inclination toward religious faith with the intensity and ferocity of some of her driven, half-crazed protagonists. What she *has* suggested repeatedly is that, in an age which has tended to discount altogether the need for redemption as conceived by a Christian under-standing of existence, a novelist whose vision is Chris-tian "may well be forced to take ever more violent means to get his vision across to [his] hostile audience. . . . To the hard of hearing you shout, and for the almost-blind you draw large and startling figures." [12] Old Mason Tarwater is a "large and startling picture," and though Miss O'Connor admitted that she considered him the hero of *The Violent Bear It Away* and that she was "right behind him 100 per cent." [13] I find nothing in the novel or in her statements about it which implies that she intended him to be taken as a model of the Chris-tian life.

There are, moreover, ways of stating the question of freedom posed by the novel so that Tarwater's decision may be considered more than simply the foreordained choice of a fanatic. Writing in rebuttal of the charges of determinism leveled against *The Violent* by Robert Bowen, Sister M. Simon Nolde provides an explication of what Flannery O'Connor apparently meant when she spoke of integrity often residing "in what [one] is not able to do":

The Violent Bear It Away not only comments on the absurdities committed in the contemporary world by those who have eyes and ears but neither see nor hear; it also comments on the way of faith as a progressive journey. As those who awaken to the full responsibility of the Christian vocation know, the response to the invitation can vary or progress from violent rejection to a grudging and, finally, to a willing acceptance. *Submission, as well as deliberate choice or rejection is a response of a free creature.*[14]

The introduction of the concept of submission, as distinct from "deliberate choice or rejection," makes possible a broader and psychologically more profound discussion of the problem of freedom than Mr. Lorch's stark either/or allows. That is, given the ineluctable and abiding influences of the conditions into which one is born (Tillich's "destiny"), how many choices for self-definition are, realistically, available to the self? Surely the findings of depth psychology have shown irrefutably that while one may reject his past, he can never completely escape it, since in the very process of rejecting, one tends to define himself *negatively* in terms of that past (Rayber provides an excellent example of this phenomenon). Moreover, since the formative experiences of one's childhood are indelibly impressed upon the unconscious, is it not possible that in attempting to extirpate them completely, one may do violence to that core of the self which is the source of one's identity (Hazel Motes seems to illustrate this principle)? When the problem is stated this way, it is no longer necessary to reject the premise that there are in human beings many conflicting wills and that submitting to what is most powerful in one's heritage, uniting one's self, as it were, may be the closest approach to freedom. Mr. Lorch maintains that Tarwater "must choose between becoming himself and becoming, in effect, his great-uncle." But this is grossly to oversimplify both the nature of human freedom and Tarwater's peculiar dilemma. It is nearer the truth to say that the boy must choose between becoming his uncle or becoming his great-uncle, although to be strictly accurate I should say that he faces the choice of self-understanding either in terms associated with Rayber or in terms associated with the old prophet. The self does not come into being by special creation *ex nihilo* but rather by means of a complex and extended cumulative process involving a diversity of influences, often conflicting ones. And what the self chooses to become and to do is, therefore, inescapably related to, though not entirely determined by, those influences. In this case, Tarwater chooses to be, creates himself, in terms of the image of selfhood which exercises the greater sway over him, this being the image of the old man, whose "domain," it has been remarked, "is the child's unconscious mind." [15]

The act which makes Tarwater's choice irrevocable is, of course, his baptismal drowning of the idiot Bishop. And though the drowning appears to be evidence of Tarwater's having succumbed at last to the demonic promptings of his "friend," one critic has argued that it is just this willingness to act as a "self-responsible" agent, to run the risk of damnation if need be, that makes Tarwater a fit vessel for the terrifying "inevitable loving wrath of God." [16] This interpretation is persuasive, especially since it illuminates the apparent positive valuation of "spiritual crime" which Miss O'Connor's fiction often suggests. Yet the expression, "the inevitable loving wrath of God," raises a vexing question about the nature of divine love as depicted in the novel. Louis Rubin, Jr. deals with this question in an essay devoted largely to an examination of the relationship between Flannery O'Connor's Roman Catholicism and the evangelical Protestantism of the South. Singling out *The Violent Bear It Away* for close explication, he contends that the issue in this book is not so much the contest of theism and atheistic rationalism as it is the sundering of divine love and wrath in Southern fundamentalist religion. Rayber, Rubin believes, fears and distrusts emotion because, for him, emotion is invariably associated with old Mason Tarwater's violence and passion. And, since he recognizes that his uncle's fanaticism is an ever-threatening potentiality within himself, he guards against its eruption by suppressing emotion in all its forms. Hence he is particularly ill-equipped to rescue young Tarwater from the hold which the old man has upon him, for what the boy requires above all else is love. But Rayber finds "overmastering love . . . as dangerous as hatred" [17] (it is hatred, Rubin feels, which lies at the heart of the old prophet's violence and wrath), and for this reason he rejects love (symbolized in Bishop) just as he is incapable of responding with love to Tarwater at those moments when the boy is most receptive.

One such moment occurs midway through the novel when the schoolteacher secretly follows Tarwater along the back streets of the city to a revival meeting. While the boy enters the mission church, Rayber peers through a window and listens as a beautiful girl, a child-preacher, expounds the love of God.

"Do you know who Jesus is?" she cried. "Jesus is the word of God and Jesus is love. The Word of God is love and do you know what love is, you people? If you don't know what love is you won't know Jesus when He comes. You won't be ready. I want to tell you people the story of the world, how it never known when love come, so when love comes again, you'll be ready." (P. 382)

Rayber's initial response to the child is outrage that she should be so exploited, but soon he is overcome by a

feeling of pity and a sense that some extraordinary communication is taking place between them. "Her dark
gaze moved slowly until it rested on Rayber's head in
the window. . . . A deep shock went through him. He
was certain that the child had looked directly into his
heart and seen his pity. He felt that some mysterious
connection was established between them" (383). Rayber feels "his spirit borne aloft" as the child preaches of
the slaughter of the Innocents and of the Word of God
as "a burning Word." As her gaze becomes riveted upon
his face, he is convinced that "[this] child alone in the
world was meant to understand him" and finds himself
silently pleading, "Come away with me! . . . and I will
teach you the truth, I'll save you, beautiful child!"
(384). For a moment lost in a rhapsodic, almost mystical experience of loving identity with the child, Rayber
is abashed and completely unstrung when the child
points him out as an example of a "dead man" whom
Jesus has not yet raised (385).

This episode is a critical one, whose importance has
sometimes been overlooked by interpreters of the novel.
For when Tarwater leaves the church and is approached
by his uncle, the boy indicates in a number of ways a
readiness, here manifest for the first time, to establish a
relationship with the schoolteacher on a basis quite different from the hostility and scorn which has dominated
his attitude to this point. In Mr. Rubin's opinion, it is

> precisely the little girl's message of a God of love that
> had almost broken the spell of the great-uncle's fanaticism
> over Tarwater; had Rayber been able to realize this, had
> he sought then to replace the mission of fanatical hate
> that the old man had instilled in Tarwater—"The Lord
> is preparing a prophet with fire in his hand and eye and
> the prophet is moving toward the city with his warning"
> . . . with the joy of God's love and mercy, he could have
> saved the youth from his fate.[18]

But Rayber is too much a victim of his own confused feelings, his own divided identity, to be able to discern or respond to Tarwater's new-found willingness to accept his uncle as the friend and father the schoolteacher had earlier offered to become. Immediately after the child Lucette points her condemning finger at him, Rayber undergoes a shock of recognition when he realizes the extent of his "loathing for the boy" (385), loathing prompted by his awareness that it is Tarwater who had lured him into this humiliating and terrifying situation.

Rubin emphasizes that Rayber is unable to react creatively to the signs of his young nephew's desire for companionship and trust "[n]ot simply from embarrassment; rather, it is because Rayber had done the one thing he fears most of all doing. Listening to the little girl, he had forgotten his sophisticated rationalism and had given way to an emotional response." [19] But it is significant that while listening to the child, Rayber's mind reverts repeatedly to scenes from his own childhood, especially to the episode involving his "rescue" from Powderhead by his unbelieving father. We recall that, at the age of seven, when Rayber had been kidnapped by his uncle Mason, the boy had come to believe the old man's message, had been baptized by him, and had, in effect, "adopted" the prophet as his father. Furthermore, when his real father had gruffly snatched him away from Powderhead, growling into his ear " 'Back to the real world, boy . . . back to the real world. And that's me and not him, see?' " Rayber had shouted in reply, " 'It's him! Him! Him and not you! And I've been born again and there's not a thing you can do about it!' " (381). Quite clearly Rayber had experienced then a trauma which plagues him for the remainder of his life. Since we learn of this experience through flashbacks interspersed among descriptions of

Rayber's loving response to the child-preacher, I think it equally clear that Rayber *sees himself in the child Lucette.* This is made explicit at one point: "His pity encompassed all exploited children—himself when he was a child, Tarwater, exploited by the old man, this child exploited by parents" (383). Here he is apparently thinking of himself as the victim of the old prophet's fantasies. A bit further on, however, Rayber again appears to conceive himself and the child to be one, and on this occasion it would seem that he imagines himself not as the victim of his uncle's fierce ravings but rather as the ardent seven-year old believer in his healing message of God's fiery grace. The passage which I am about to quote, both in its imagery, so reminiscent of the old prophet's, and in its position—after Rayber's silent appeal to the young girl to come away with him (to another Powderhead?) where he "will teach [her] the truth" and *save* her and just before her denunciation of him as a "dead man"—suggests that more is at stake here than simply the emotional response which Rubin emphasizes.

> Her eyes still fixed on him, she cried, "I've seen the Lord in a tree of fire! The Word of God is a burning Word to burn you clean!" She was moving in his direction, the people in front of her forgotten. Rayber's heart began to race. He felt some miraculous communication between them. The child alone in the world was meant to understand him. "Burns the whole world, man and child," she cried, her eye on him, "none can escape." She stopped a little distance from the end of the stage and stood silent, her whole attention directed across the small room to his face on the ledge. *Her eyes were large and dark and fierce.* He felt that in the space between them, their spirits had broken the bonds of age and ignorance and were mingling in some unheard of knowledge of each other. He was transfixed by the child's silence [emphasis added]. (Pp. 384–85)

Listening to the child's passionate preaching, Rayber is mesmerized by her "fierce" eyes and by the mood created by her words. Both the eyes and the language recall the old prophet, and Rayber, for a brief moment, sees in the child proclaiming "[t]he Word of God [which] is a burning Word to burn you clean" both his fanatical uncle whom he claims to have repudiated and also himself as a seven-year-old boy forced out of an idyllic existence with the old man into the "real world" where he has since never once felt totally at home or secure. In short, after this experience, Rayber is too agitated to respond with kindness to Tarwater not only because he has succumbed momentarily to the temptation of emotion but also, and perhaps principally, because he has during this brief encounter felt the kind of acceptance which the old prophet had accorded him as a child, only to be rejected in the rudest and cruelest fashion. The imagery of Rayber's fantasizing about taking the child away and saving her strongly suggests just such a paradise as Powderhead must have seemed to Rayber the impressionable child, and therefore her rude rejection of him in proclaiming him a "dead man" might well be experienced as a reliving of the trauma of his forced ejection from that earlier Eden at the hands of his irreverent and callous father. If the validity of this interpretation be granted, Rayber's brusque handling of Tarwater and his insensitivity to the boy's expectant openness are the more understandable, rooted as they are in Rayber's feelings of loss and forlornness. Significantly, his manner of dealing with Tarwater is parallel to and reminiscent of his own father's insensitive handling of him.

Throughout the book it is evident that Rayber's relationship to his uncle is in some ways more equivocal than is young Tarwater's, and increasingly there emerges a pattern of action indicating that his efforts to root out

from the boy the influence of the old prophet constitute
in fact a desperate attempt to exorcise the "demons" he
feels have been implanted *in him*. This much is clear.
What has perhaps not been sufficiently emphasized is
that Rayber *loves* the old man with a love as strong as
his hate. When, therefore, he is rejected by the child
Lucette in language which Masòn Tarwater himself
might have employed, the psychological force of this
event may be even more powerfully related to his uncle
than to his father, since with the uncle is associated a
love which he desperately needs and desperately fears.

I have examined this episode in considerable detail
because, while I agree in large part with Mr. Rubin's
analysis of its significance, it appears to me that his
interpretation does not do full justice to its complexity.
First of all, his treatment of Rayber's response to the
child's preaching explains that response in terms of
Rayber's fear of emotion, but fails to take into account
the reasons for the schoolteacher's very genuine attraction to and identification with the child and the pain he
suffers in her harsh rejection. Secondly, in emphasizing
Lucette's message of God's love, Mr. Rubin apparently
ignores the fact that, as proclaimed by the child-
preacher, God's love is no less intertwined with His
wrath than it is in the message of the old prophet. The
child states that "The Word of God is love" and proceeds to ask the congregation if they know "what love
is." Yet the only answer that she offers is couched in
language quite compatible with that which the old
prophet had used in his own proclamations and denun-
ciations: " 'The Word of God is a burning Word to
burn you clean' " (384). Thus it is conceivable, if not
probable, that when Tarwater leaves the mission church
we may not assume, as Rubin does, that "the little girl's
message of a God of love . . . [has] almost broken the
spell of the great-uncle's fanaticism. . . ." Indeed, the

description of the boy's manner of greeting Rayber would tend to suggest that the child's message has had the effect of reinforcing the influence of the old prophet: "he raised his arm in an uncertain gesture of greeting. *The sight of Rayber seemed to afford him relief amounting to rescue*" [emphasis added] (385). Tarwater, in other words, looks to Rayber to rescue him from the influence of the old prophet because, having succumbed to the extent of visiting the Pentecostal Tabernacle and having been shaken in spite of himself by the child's preaching, he now realizes how *un*free he is of his great-uncle's power. But Rayber is no less unfree and the crucial opportunity is lost.

It has been said of Tarwater that "[he] wants to love, but he has been taught only to hate." [20] It is an error, however, to locate the source of hate and destruction exclusively in old Mason Tarwater, thus ignoring the influence upon Rayber, and hence indirectly upon Tarwater, of Rayber's unfeeling, spiritually bankrupt father. Rayber is completely incapacitated for becoming an effectual guide and father-substitute to Tarwater because he too has never known any love except the irrational "longing . . . like an undertow in his blood" associated with the old man and his "impossible vision of a world transfigured." And, understandably, Rayber must combat this longing since he has grounds for fearing that yielding to it will lead almost inevitably to madness.

But this should not blind us to the fact that it is not Tarwater alone who hates. Rayber also hates, the difference being that Tarwater is more honest and open about his hating. As we saw, after the experience at the gospel temple, Rayber is overcome by a "loathing for the boy that earlier would have made him shudder" (385). And his loathing is clearly not associated with the old prophet's irrationalism but rather with the rationalism by means of which he hopes to hold it in check: "[the overpowering love] began with Bishop and then like an avalanche covered everything his reason hated" (372). From this I would conclude that if it may be asserted that the conflict in Tarwater is between "the creative, life-giving emotion of love and the destructive, death-bringing emotion of hatred and violence," [21] the same conflict exists covertly in Rayber, and for the destructive emotion of hatred the "violently" profane father is at least as responsible as the violently religious uncle.

Rubin, in effect, implies this causal connection when he says, "In a world in which 'faith supported by love' cannot survive the attack of secular materialism, only faith achieved through hatred is possible," [22] although here, of course, he has in mind Tarwater, not Rayber. Obviously, Rayber achieves no faith, nor does he learn to accept or give love. Clearly he too has been "warped" by the fanaticism of the old prophet. But his inability to save Tarwater by means of a gospel of love, as well as his (partially) self-inflicted dehumanization, cannot be laid entirely to the charge of his great-uncle, as Rubin's thesis is inclined to imply. Love and wrath may indeed be sundered in Southern evangelical religion, but the novel itself suggests that whatever Rayber may know of love, he has learned from his primitive fundamentalist uncle and not from his secularized "civilized" father.

I would add that what has been declared true of Tarwater—that he "is not *fated* to take up the old man's burden of prophecy; he does so because the world, and not fate, compels him to it" [23]—is true, *mutatis mutandis*, of Rayber: he too is not fated to be an unloving, self-pitying, ineffectual rationalist, except insofar as "the world," i.e., the peculiar matrix of psychological and spiritual forces emanating principally from his uncle and his father, has made him so. Could it not be said that Rayber and Tarwater are equally free and unfree, since both are motivated (as are all human beings) by forces outside themselves, experienced, for the most part, during childhood? The difference, as I have pointed out above, lies in Tarwater's capacity to choose and to act, to take responsibility for his action and, finally, to ground his life in *commitment to something*. And for this, it is the old prophet—wrathful, yes, and violent too—whom Tarwater must thank.

Everything That Rises Must Converge

In Flannery O'Connor's posthumous volume of stories, *Everything That Rises Must Converge* (1965), subject and setting are very much a part of the contemporary South. Economic growth is under way, and its partisans are feverishly engaged as midwives to "progress" ("A View of the Woods"); racial integration is a fact increasingly difficult to ignore, and white Southerners of all classes are forced to assume some attitude toward it ("Everything That Rises Must Converge"). The upheavals wrought by World War II and the Korean conflict have unsettled class lines, and the sons of tenant farmers are on their way to becoming "society" ("Greenleaf"); the dispersion of poor whites throughout the urban North is well advanced, constituting opportunity for many of the young but exile in an alien and hostile land for the elderly ("Judgement Day"). And, as in the novel, *The Violent Bear It Away*, the techniques of modern psychology are being liberally applied by social worker-types reared on progressive philosophies ("The Lame Shall Enter First"). Wherever one turns in these stories, he encounters evidence of Flannery O'Connor's sensitivity to the changes which her region was undergoing during the late 1950s and early 1960s.

As always, Miss O'Connor brought to these subjects an intelligence keenly alive to the complexities of the human mind—its subterfuges, its self-deceptions, its seemingly inexhaustible capacity for rationalization. In her two novels and in such early stories as "Good Country People," "The Life You Save May Be Your Own," and "The Artificial Nigger," she had demonstrated an astonishingly mature grasp of the dynamics of human psychology. Yet something new (in degree if not in kind) seems to distinguish the stories of the second collection: an almost clinical understanding of certain forms of neurosis. The title story, for example, is a virtual case study of what psychoanalysts would describe as denial and projection.

The narrative itself is simple enough: Julian and his mother travel by bus to the Y in order that she may attend a reducing class. Contemptuous of his mother, from whose values and prejudices he thinks he has freed himself, Julian attempts unsuccessfully to befriend a Negro man and indulges in malicious glee when a large Negro woman boards the bus wearing a hat identical to the one his mother has on. As they leave the bus together, Mrs. Chestny offers a penny to the Negro woman's small son and is knocked to the sidewalk by the infuriated Negress. After pointing out to his mother that she has been taught a proper lesson, Julian discovers that she is dying and runs for help in a last futile effort to delay his entrance in the "world of guilt and sorrow." [1]

Like many of the sad young men of Flannery O'Connor's last stories, the protagonist of "Everything That Rises Must Converge" wants desperately to distinguish himself from everything in the South which he finds morally, intellectually, and aesthetically repugnant: its racism, its nostalgia for the glorious past, its (to him) petty concern with manners, its barren intellectual life, its insufferably banal social intercourse. (Julian is cast from the same mold that produced the rebellious "artistic" or "intellectual" sons of "The Enduring Chill," "The Comforts of Home," and "Greenleaf." Julian, Asbury, Thomas, and Wesley make up a quartet of angry, frustrated individuals caught in "late adolescent" impotence so acute that they can direct their hostility only against their protective, and oftentimes patronizing and controlling mothers.)

Julian wants to be different, and since everything about the South which affronts his sense of decency and decorum is symbolized by his mother, Julian wants especially to be different from his mother. Merely being different, however, is not sufficient; his hatred for all that his mother epitomizes is so venomous that he must constantly insult it. As it is impossible to insult the entire Southern ethos, Julian is reduced to the expediency of humiliating and insulting his mother. But Julian's relation to his mother, like his relation to the South itself, is less unambiguous than he would like to imagine. What he thinks he detests, he also loves and longs for. What he believes he is totally free of, he is, in fact, fearfully dependent upon.

While Miss O'Connor undoubtedly portrays the bad faith of Julian as the more damning, it must be conceded that there is something exasperating about his mother. She is one of those legendary Southern matrons of "aristocratic" birth who, though forced to live in relative poverty, continues to insist upon a distinction which she believes birth has conferred upon her. Though she must use the now-integrated public transportation system and must associate at the YWCA with women of a lower social class, she insists that because she " 'knows who she is,' " she " 'can be gracious to anybody' " (6). Indeed, it is this assumption that the glue which holds society together is a certain politeness and openness of manner—almost always, however, practiced with a degree of unconscious condescension—which enables

Julian's mother to face the unpleasant alterations in her external circumstances with a calm and cheerful assurance that she herself at least has not changed. It is her ardent faith in the primacy of manners, in fact, which is one of the sources of the conflict between Julian and his mother. She insists that authentic culture is " 'in the heart . . . and in how you do things and how you do things is because of who you *are*' " (9). Julian's attitude provides the starkest contrast, since he maintains that with the new fluidity of class structure, his mother's graciousness counts for nothing. " 'Knowing who you are is good for one generation only,' " he declares. " 'You haven't the foggiest idea where you stand now or who you are' " (6).

Naturally, Julian is convinced that he knows where *he* is. Yet he is in fact far more pitifully confused than his mother. In him Flannery O'Connor has drawn a devastating portrait of the young white "liberal" Southerner who is doing all of the supposedly right things for the wrong reasons. Conceited in his assurance that he is free of his mother's prejudices and her unrealistic attachment to a dead past, Julian betrays in every gesture and word his thoroughly ambivalent attitudes toward the principal objects of her bigotry (Negroes) and her nostalgia (the ancestral home). How small the distance is he has put between himself and the heritage which he condemns is suggested in this description of his feelings about the family mansion he had once seen as a child.

> He never spoke of it without contempt or thought of it without longing. He had seen it once . . . . The double stairways had rotted and been torn down. Negroes were living [in] it. But it remained in his mind as his mother had known it. It appeared in his dreams regularly. . . . He preferred its threadbare elegance to anything he could name. (Pp. 7–8)

In some way reminiscent of Quentin Compson's tortured exclamation at the conclusion of *Absalom,*

Absalom!, "I don't hate it, I don't hate it" (the "it" referring to the South), Julian's reveries reflect much of the ambivalence but little of the profundity of Quentin's attitude toward the traditional South. For, whereas Quentin stands much closer to the great decisive events which have shaped Southern history and must grapple existentially with their meaning, as well as with the meaning of his own family's former glory and present decadence, Julian is a child of the 1950s and sixties, and, as such, faces the quite different problem of establishing personal identity in a South for which neither the grandeur nor the guilt of the past are ever-present, haunting realities. Yet the tradition which his mother represents, while attenuated and diluted, is nonetheless a factor with which he must reckon. Wishing to assert his independence from his mother, he vehemently proclaims his independence of the cultural heritage from which she derives *her* identity. But as he finds his present life and surroundings drab and humiliating, he is forced against his conscious will to identify with that very way of life which he can neither appropriate completely, as his mother thinks she has done, nor repudiate completely, as he would like to believe he has done.

The confusion of his attitude toward the Southern past is recapitulated and underscored in his ambivalent feelings toward his mother, whom he considers a child, "innocent and untouched by experience," for whose protection he must sacrifice himself. Remote as Julian's mother's world may be from reality, Julian's own fantasy world is even more remote. With his arrogant sense of superiority ("he realized he was too intelligent to be a success" [11]), Julian's habitual way of dealing with the unpleasant aspects of life is to retreat "into the inner compartment of his mind . . . a kind of mental bubble" from which he may judge the intellectual bankruptcy of the rest of mankind. Somewhat like Hulga

and very much like Asbury of "The Enduring Chill,"
Wesley of "Greenleaf," and Thomas of "The Comforts
of Home," Julian suffers from a form of neurosis in
which his idealized image is threatened by self-doubt
and self-pity and can be protected only by maintaining
an uncommitted and superior attitude toward the world.
At the same time subjecting the world to withering
scorn for its failures and fearing to engage the world in
creative struggle, Julian withdraws into his bubble where
the self is free to judge without making itself vulnerable
to judgment.

The viability of Julian's defensive psychological mechanism largely depends upon the availability of someone
whom he can continuously belittle and scorn and whose
stupidity and phoniness (as judged by him) can serve
to point up, by contrast, his own supposedly enlightened
and authentic existence. And that person is his mother.
But while Julian thus needs his mother, she also poses a
constant threat, to the extent that she is able to with-
stand his attacks and, through simply being what she is,
to insinuate the possibility of some radical discrepancy
between his idealized image and the actuality of his life.
Ultimately, therefore, he must attempt to destroy her
or destroy *for* her that system of values which makes her
life possible.

On the bus an opportunity of attack presents itself
when a white woman moves from a seat next to one just
occupied by a Negro man. Ostensibly to "convey his
sympathy" but actually to embarrass his mother, Julian
crosses the aisle to the vacated seat. Now so situated that
he can stare at her as though he were a stranger, Julian
experiences a release of tension such as might accompany a declaration of war (13). Julian now fantasizes
about various ways of hurting his mother, though always
the conscious intention is "to teach her a lesson." Interestingly, all of his schemes involve Negroes or causes
related to Negroes.

Here brief reflection upon Julian's "liberalism" should help to illumine the moral and psychological ramifications of the story. It is clear that Julian uses his putative tolerance and freedom from racial bias as a weapon in the struggle with his mother. What is far worse, he *uses Negroes* for the same purpose. Significantly, Julian has "never been successful in making Negro friends" (15); the reason for his failure is not difficult to locate, since he all too obviously wishes only to accumulate "some of the better types, . . . ones that looked like professors or ministers or lawyers" (15) to bolster his always tenuous hold upon his self-image as a liberated representative of the "new South." Julian's own latent prejudice begins to show itself when a huge, fierce-looking Negro woman, who could not possibly be mistaken for a member of the Negro intelligentsia, boards the bus and settles in a seat next to his. Julian is "annoyed." Quickly his annoyance turns to elation as he sees the symbolic appropriateness of the two women having "swapped sons" when the woman's small child sits next to his mother. Julian's triumph is completed when he notices that the Negro woman's hat is an exact match of the one his mother is wearing for the first time.

Reveling briefly in his mother's distress, Julian discovers their true relationship after she has been struck to the ground by the hostile Negro woman. Attempting to reinforce the "lesson" with what sounds like a rehearsed lecture, Julian assures his mother that the fury she has just witnessed is not that of a single "uppity Negro woman" but rather that of "the whole colored race which will no longer take your condescending pennies" (21). His speech is lost on his mother, who, calling for "Grampa" and Caroline (the Negro mammy who had cared for her as a child), willingly submits to "a tide of darkness" which carries her swiftly back to the ordered world of childhood and thence to death. Julian, who had moments before wished to prove to his

mother she could not expect to be forever dependent
upon him, is compelled at last to recognize how total
has been his dependence upon her. Crying "Mamma,
Mamma!" he throws himself beside her, but "Mamma,"
whose gaze had earlier scanned his face but recognized
nothing there, lies motionless. Last seen racing toward
lights which appear to recede beyond his grasp, Julian
postpones momentarily "his entry into the world of
guilt and sorrow" (23). On this unmistakable Haw-
thornesque note the chronicle of another American
Adam is concluded.

For a number of reasons the choice of this story to
open the collection was a happy one. Like the stories
examined in the chapter on *A Good Man Is Hard to
Find* and like most of the stories in this volume, "Everything That Rises Must Converge" focuses upon the
existential dilemmas of the self—its anxiety before the
truth of its condition, the contemptible dodges it em-
ploys to deceive itself, and the inescapable surge of
guilt as the shock of awareness is delivered. But in this
tale the social context is broadened, thereby providing a
connecting thread to the last story in *A Good Man Is
Hard to Find*, "The Displaced Person," in which race
relations play a significant role, as well as pointing forward to the other pieces in the present volume, in most
of which there is a heightened consciousness of the
social ambience within which the awakened individual
must live in the presence of grace. Both the title and
the story's action give evidence of Flannery O'Connor's
growing interest in the movement of the isolated self
toward union with others; and while many commentators have maintained that Miss O'Connor uses the
line borrowed from Teilhard de Chardin ironically, I
find myself in agreement with those critics who contend
that in the narrative of Julian and his mother there is a
true convergence, although not a simple one. As the

title suggests, the story concerns both rising and converging. Before their bus ride, Julian's mother had spoken of the propriety of Negroes rising, "but on their side of the fence." Her encounter with the outraged woman attests to the rising which has already occurred, as well as the fragility of the fence and the difficulty of maintaining it. But a convergence, albeit a violent one, does take place, and there are numerous hints besides the obvious one of the identical hats, that Julian's mother and the Negro woman are more alike than either would care to admit. If nothing else, the story's action foreshadows a convergence such as that envisaged by Teilhard, who speaks of "courage and resourcefulness" as necessary ingredients in the struggle to overcome "the forces of isolationism, even of repulsion, which seem to drive [men] apart rather than draw them together." [2] Though the results of this particular convergence are quite the opposite of those anticipated by Teilhard when mankind achieves its unity in Christ, and though it would seem that here there is only reinforced isolation and repulsion, emphasis should perhaps be placed upon the pain and cost of both rising and converging. Such emphasis is certainly congruent with Miss O'Connor's belief that redemption is never easy and always involves suffering. The frustration and anger of the Negro woman *and* her courage imply a depth of spirit out of which might someday come the "resourcefulness" requisite for genuine convergence.

But since it is Julian, not the Negro mother, who is the main character, it is his rising and convergence which is central. As in other renditions of the fortunate fall, Julian's calamity will eventually lead, so all the evidence indicates, to "growth of consciousness," to raised sight, to a risen spirit. According to Teilhard de Chardin, growth toward unity with others is the spiritual direction of evolution and is a process to which those with "expanded consciousness" contribute. It is, moreover, the true end of man. "To be *fully* ourselves it is in . . . the direction of convergence with all the rest, that we must advance—towards the 'other.' " [3] Teilhard distinguishes between individuality and personhood and asserts that the latter can be achieved only by "uniting together. . . . The true ego grows in inverse proportion to 'egoism.' " [4] Insofar as Julian is able to replace his defensive idealized image with a realistic view of the self which obviates the necessity of belittling others in order to enhance the value of the self, to this extent will it be possible for him to attain personhood, a "true ego" capable of proper self-love and proper love of others. The capacity to develop such an ego is the psychological equivalent of the Christian's faith in man's ability to be radically altered by grace, and in the volume as a whole this capacity emerges as a central concern.

One critic offers a useful clue to the basis of these stories' commonly acknowledged excellence when he observes that "[i]t is as though in the struggle against her illness [Flannery O'Connor] had come to locate grotesqueness and grace in the common life of men and that she had no more time or talent to waste on merely being odd or bizarre." [5] Here one may feel compelled to demur, since today most critics agree that even in her earliest fiction Flannery O'Connor spent little of her time on the *merely* odd or bizarre. Yet this reviewer has put his finger on something real and important in the development of Miss O'Connor's talent: in the last stories she has apparently left behind the blatant melodrama of, say, "A Good Man is Hard to Find." Her Misfits are no longer psychopathic killers or voyeuristic Bible salesmen. They are instead the ineffectual sons of well-meaning but exasperating mothers. Or they are the emotionally disturbed Wellesley student and the self-righteous Mrs. Turpin of "Revelation." Exceptions there are, two or three stories which demonstrate Flannery O'Connor's penchant for the extreme situation and the exaggerated character—for instance, "Parker's Back" and "The Lame Shall Enter First." But for the most part she did seem to find her imagination creating less extravagantly fanciful characters than Tom T. Shiftlet or Manley Pointer or Hazel Motes. More often than not, too, it is in the "common life of men" that she located the workings of grace. Which is not to say that there is anything commonplace or tame about the stories in *Everything That Rises*; on the contrary, here is abundant grotesquerie and violence. Instead of abandoning altogether her taste for melodrama, "she severely disciplined it to weight the consequences of perverse will and crooked passions," [6] the result being that in such a story as "A View of the Woods," what appears as a more or less harmless and humorous contest of wills detonates into a fury of destruction, and self-destruction, even as the comic surface is preserved almost to the very end.

The action is easily summarized: an old man, Mark Fortune, permits his son-in-law Pitts, whom he detests, to farm his property; but, from time to time, largely to provoke his daughter and her family, Mr. Fortune sells off a lot. The only member of the Pitts family the old man can tolerate is the youngest daughter, Mary Fortune, who bears an uncanny likeness to her grandfather and whom he considers virtually an extension of himself. These two form an invincible alliance against the Pitts clan until the old man conceives the idea of selling the land directly in front of the house. Since Mary Fortune has heretofore shared his enthusiasm for "progress," the old man assumes that she will be free of what is to him an irrational Pitts attachment to the land. To his dismay he learns that on this issue Mary Fortune sides with her family, and, in the story's denouement, he attempts to punish her physically for opposing his scheme. Having counted on neither her ferocity nor her strength, the old man finds himself overpowered by the girl, and it is only when she releases her hold that he is able to subdue her. Inadvertently, he strikes her head against a rock, killing her, and then himself dies of a heart attack.

This bare outline, of course, provides no indication of the comedy of the piece. Neither does it allow for more than a hint of its tragic dimensions. Presumably it was a failure to discern these tragic elements which led Stanley Hyman to the otherwise mystifying conclusion that the ending involves "the unnecessary multiple death of Jacobean drama." [7] Obviously, if Miss O'Connor intended this as merely a comic story, the deaths are not only unnecessary but downright inappropriate. What seems to be the case, however, is that "A View of the Woods" is an example of that modern genre which Flannery O'Connor practices with considerable success —the story with a comic (or "absurd") surface beneath which lies a feeling for the human reality which approaches the tragic.

Mark Fortune, the story's protagonist, most certainly exhibits traits usually associated with the hero of traditional tragedy. He is a man whose sense of self is magnified to the point of becoming monstrous. He cannot tolerate criticism, claims a godlike omniscience with respect to the thoughts and feelings of others, meets opposition with unhesitating action and unswerving faith in the correctness of his judgment. He considers himself on the side of Fate or the gods (in this case, "progress") and aspires to immortal glory (a town to be named after him). His excessive and misplaced confidence in the justice of his cause and in the power of his will to implement that cause leads to events which shatter his project and destroy both himself and the chosen agent of his dream. Finally, in the moment of death, Mark Fortune, the proud tyrant of a cherished if insignificant kingdom, perceives both the mocking emptiness of his life and the fatality which has lain hidden behind the façade of his willful rationalizations and self-justifications. Mark Fortune is no Oedipus or Hamlet, and perhaps he lacks the tragic (or tragicomic) potential of even a Hazel Motes. Yet he is anything but a "perfect comic" character, and his violent death is, as I shall show, the only fitting conclusion (dramatically as well as morally) to this story of monstrous egotism and haughty disdain for the feelings and rights of others.

An extremely self-centered and possessive man, Mr. Fortune had apparently resented his daughter's marrying—at any rate, marrying the "idiot" Pitts. Hence, when she comes home with her none-too-successful husband and seven children, "she [comes] back like any other tenant" (56). Of Mary Fortune, he makes a conspicuous exception as she has "his intelligence, his strong will, and his push and drive." But his feeling for her transcends mere respect or affection. For in the nine-year-old child Mr. Fortune sees so much of himself that she represents for him the hope of an almost literal reincarnation. When he is dead and can no longer torment the Pittses, Mary Fortune, he thinks, will perpetuate that source of gratification, since he has secretly left his property in trust to her.

From the old man's standpoint, one thing only mars this relationship. This is Pitts's periodic, sadistic beating of Mary Fortune for no apparent cause, and Mr. Fortune is enraged and made physically ill each time it occurs. For he conceives Pitts's aggression to be directed toward him, as clearly it is; "This was Pitts's revenge on him. It was as if it were *he* that Pitts was driving down the road to beat and as if *he* were the one submitting to it" (61–62). And each time he confronts Mary Fortune with her "cowardice," her failure to defy her father, the child emphatically repudiates his accusation, stoutly maintaining that no one has beaten her and that " 'if anyone did [she'd] kill him' " (61). Considering the extreme pain which Mary Fortune's humiliation and suffering cause him, it is a reasonable assumption that the old man's motives in taunting Pitts are colored by a tinge of masochism. But, whatever his unconscious motives, his conscious hatred of Pitts grows with each brutal assault upon Mary Fortune, causing him to seek ever more devilish ways of inflicting pain upon the child's father.

Clearly, affronting Pitts and his "tribe" satisfies some deep psychological need in the old man. So too does any act which reinforces his conviction that he, unlike the dull and backward Pitts, is on the side of "progress." Thus his eagerness to see a town arise on his property. As a beginning, he intends to sell the "lawn" to the owner of one of those combination roadside businesses— gas station, country store, dance hall and junk yard— which dot the Southern landscape. Tilman signifies for Mr. Fortune the resourceful man who goes boldly forward to meet the future, "the kind . . . who was never just in line with progress but always a little ahead of it" (67). The narrator's description of the man is more sinister and more revealing: Tilman normally sits at the counter with folded hands, "his insignificant head weaving snake-fashion above them" (76). Mr. Fortune may believe, when he signs the deed of sale, that he is dealing with an enlightened apostle of progress, but Flannery O'Connor suggests, rather too obviously perhaps, that he is signing a pact with the devil.

What is soon made evident is that he is signing his own death warrant as well. For in his refusal to heed his granddaughter's initial complaint that the "lawn" not only makes possible a view of the woods but also provides space where "[her] daddy grazes his calves," there is a foreshadowing of the fatal miscalculation which is destined to demolish all of Mr. Fortune's grand hopes. For the child is like him in so many ways that he is quite incapable of believing that, in this instance, her sympathies are with her "daddy." The irony of his position is perfect, since it is those very qualities which he most admires in the child—her independent spirit, her strong will, her obstinacy—which compel her to oppose him when he forces her to choose (" 'Are you a Fortune, he said, 'or are you a Pitts? Make up your mind' " [74]) between her family and him. In forcing this choice he is, in effect, asking her to submerge her individuality in his, something her spirited, self-assertive nature will not permit. Thus she responds to his challenge by saying she is " 'Mary—Fortune—Pitts,' " or, in other words, herself: a Pitts, with an abundance of Fortune temperament, but finally MARY—an independent self which transcends categories and clans. The old man's shouted reply, " 'Well I am PURE Fortune!' " is later echoed by the child as she sits astride his chest, having just administered him a savage pummeling: "The old man looked up into his own image. It was triumphant and hostile. 'You been whipped,' it said, 'by me' and then it added, bearing down on each word, 'and I'm PURE Pitts' " (80). Enraged to hear his "own image" claiming to be everything that he loathes, the old man takes the child by the throat and pounds her head on the ground, after which he "stare[s] at his conquered image" (80).

The language of this and other passages intensifies the impression of Mark Fortune as a deeply troubled and divided man. His inordinate identification with the child clearly indicates that she fills the role of his double. Yet, when their basic interests conflict, he learns to his dismay that she embodies not only that part of himself which he admires but also another, unacknowledged and suppressed aspect of his humanity. The child stands for a quality of imagination and sensibility which can recognize in ordinary pine trees some of the glory and wonder of nature, the loss of which no amount of "progress" can compensate for. That quality, atrophied and nearly extinct in himself, still lives feebly on in the deepest recesses of his unconscious mind, and when it threatens to interfere with his conscious purposes, he acts (as if by compulsion) to destroy it. Hence his killing of Mary Fortune, while not a consciously willed act, corresponds to a profound conflict within his unconscious. Her death symbolizes a violent extirpation of a part of himself and it is indeed his own "conquered image" which he beholds as he stares at his lifeless granddaughter.

The story's imagery illumines this division within the old man's psyche. There are two primary and opposing patterns, corresponding to the two dimensions of Mr. Fortune's self. The first of these patterns consists of images of mechanisms, is associated with the old man's belief in progress, and is represented chiefly by the earthmoving machine which is digging an artificial lake. This machine is portrayed as if it were some living, mindless creature compelled endlessly to devour and then disgorge the earth. Like her grandfather, Mary Fortune is enthralled by its activities; both are depicted as "looking down into the red pit, watching the big disembodied gullet gorge itself on the clay, then, with the sound of a deep sustained nausea and a slow mechanical revulsion, turn and spit it up" (55). The machine seems intended to symbolize a malignancy, a repulsive disease in the old man or in the dream of progress to which he is so compulsively committed. Its description as a "disembodied gullet" conjures up a picture of grotesque, unnatural voraciousness, while the phrases "sustained nausea" and "mechanical revulsion" suggest a form of nonintelligent resistance to the ceaseless gorging. Interestingly, there are links between the two symbols of "progress," the machine and the Snopes-like Tilman: both are portrayed as reptilian (Tilman as snake, the earth mover as perhaps mechanical dinosaur), both as devourers without intelligent purpose. Correspondingly, the old man's obsessive pursuit of the future, in utter disregard of the feelings of those closest to him, is an analogue of the mindless rapacity of the machine.

The images of the second pattern are drawn from nature, the central image in this configuration being the woods themselves. In contrast to the machine, the woods are pictured as lifelike, virtually human. The distinction is established early: the already examined passage describing the machine is from the story's third paragraph; in the first paragraph the reader is told that the lake construction is "bordered on [one] side by a black line of woods which appeared at both ends of the view to walk across the water" (54). Near the middle of the story, Mary Fortune rejects her grandfather's efforts at reconciliation, all the while staring across the front lot to the distant trees and looking "into this scene *as if it were a person* that she preferred to him" [emphasis added] (70). Disgusted with her behavior, Mr. Fortune enters the house for his afternoon rest. Twice he goes to the window and each time sees "just woods."

> The third time he got up to look at the woods, . . . the gaunt trunks appeared to be raised in a pool of red light that gushed from the almost hidden sun setting behind them. The old man stared for some time, as if for a prolonged instant he were caught up out of the rattle of everything that led to the future and were held there in the midst of an uncomfortable mystery that he had not apprehended before. He saw it, in his hallucination, as if someone were wounded behind the woods and the trees were bathed in blood. After a few minutes this

unpleasant vision was broken by the presence of Pitt's pick-up truck grinding to a halt below the window. (P. 71)

In this crucial passage it becomes apparent that, through the medium of the woods, some elemental and persistent component of reality is attempting to communicate with the old man and that he finds this inchoate communication unsettling and threatening. His fixation upon the future is momentarily suspended as a force deep within himself enters into a kind of mystical communion with a force in nature. But the mystery is too "uncomfortable" to be long endured, and the old man is soon snatched back into the safe and familiar world of mechanism by the "grinding" of Pitt's truck. The experience, however, has penetrated his defenses, the magnitude of its threat being disclosed by the extravagance of the rationalizations to which he is driven later that evening.

The conflict symbolized by the machine/woods opposition is brought to a climax in the final paragraph. Mary Fortune lies motionless on the ground; next to her lies the old man, whose heart, threatening to give way throughout the narrative, at last succumbs to the excitement of his violent encounter with the child. Again a "vision" forces itself upon his imagination and this time he perceives, too late, the meaning of the trees and machine and, thus, the meaning of his life. Feeling himself pulled along toward the water and desperate to escape the encircling woods (always, in an O'Connor story, a sign of the presence of grace), the old man imagines himself about to be enfolded by the lake's miniature waves. He remembers that he cannot swim, and then the trees, which earlier had seemed "ugly," begin to thicken "into mysterious dark files" and march away "across the water," leaving him utterly alone "except for one huge yellow monster . . . gorging itself on clay" (81).

The significance of the "huge yellow monster" is evident; the symbolism of the trees requires further investigation. Sister Bernetta Quinn has written that "the woods . . . represent those moments of grace, of inspiration, which come to all of us from time to time." [8] But since the old man rejects this grace, to him the woods are "first of all a vision of hell." [9] This conclusion is undoubtedly suggested by the consummation of the old man's vision on the previous afternoon when, after looking at the woods three times, he returns to bed and then "against [his] closed lids hellish red trunks [rise] up in a black wood" (71). Moments earlier, however, the "uncomfortable mystery" had been bodied forth in a different guise: "He saw it . . . as if someone were wounded behind the woods and the trees were bathed in blood" (71). In this trope and in the incident when Mary Fortune stares at the woods as though she were seeing a person, the trees take on attributes of the human. But, as Sister Bernetta's remarks imply, we seem here to be dealing with the human extended to that limit of height or depth where "human" and "divine" meet and fuse. The moment in history when this meeting was most radically concretized is recalled, I think, in the imagery of "the gaunt trees [which appear] to be raised in a pool of red light that gushed from the almost hidden sun . . . ." But, whether it is Christ's crucifixion which is being recollected in the figure of the trees "bathed in blood" or Mary Fortune's or his own death which is being foreshadowed, the story's ending leaves no doubt that in repudiating the trees and the "grace" which they symbolize, Mr. Fortune has chosen for himself a lonely, despairing death.

This ending may be melodramatic; but, then, so also is that of *Doctor Faustus*. And the vision of damnation, while patently more modern than that of Marlowe's play, is scarcely less terrifying. The comparison, in fact, is not altogether gratuitous. For, like Faustus in his uncompromising pursuit of knowledge and power, Mr. Fortune allows his blind passion for the dream of "progress" to destroy the agents necessary for the realization of that dream—Mary Fortune and himself. But his true tragedy (and again the analogy with Faustus is surprisingly apt) resides in the fact that his dream is of such a nature that its "success" depends upon the destruction of a faculty within himself which, though suppressed and underdeveloped, is nevertheless essential for his existence as a whole human being. Only in his dying moments, when the "gaunt trees" have "thickened into mysterious dark files," only when these signs of the deep mystery surrounding man's life (and invulnerable to his rapacious gorging) have deserted him, does Mark Fortune come to a full recognition of the sterility and dehumanized bleakness of his dream.

Almost every critic who has commented on Flannery O'Connor's novella "The Lame Shall Enter First" has noted its similarities to *The Violent Bear It Away,* published two years earlier. In the shorter work the trio of characters from the novel—Rayber, Bishop, and Tarwater—are metamorphosed into a social worker, Sheppard, his not overly bright child, Norton, and Rufus Johnson, a clubfooted juvenile delinquent with a missionary zeal to expose his "tin Jesus" benefactor for the sham that he is. As in the novel, the child dies, the rebellious teen-ager wins the struggle with the "positivist" adult, while the latter discovers, in a convulsive moment of self-revelation, the hollowness of his soul. In other ways, too, the works are alike: Sheppard shares Rayber's belief in the power of rational understanding over irrational impulse, and the action of the story is generated, in large part, by his effort to prove true Rayber's dictum that "[w]hat we understand we can control." Rufus, the recalcitrant youth, like Tarwater, has imbibed from a fanatical grandfather a great religious passion, though in his case the satanical and criminal element is overt and pronounced. To Sheppard's bland assertions that Rufus can make of himself anything he sets his mind to, the boy retorts, tauntingly and mockingly, " 'Satan . . . has me in his power' " (150). Rufus also differs from Tarwater in another respect, for he is without any ambivalence toward his would-be "savior": from the beginning he feels only contempt, and when he does occasionally express toward Sheppard some slight trust and affection, he is all the while slyly baiting a trap.

There are other important ways in which the two works differ, one of the chief being the nature of the central conflict in each. As we saw, the Rayber-Tarwater conflict involves principally the clash of a positivist world view and an understanding of reality which allows for something "left over" after man's abstracting intellect has exhausted its potency. This theme is also present in "The Lame Shall Enter First," but the novella is much more than a simple reworking of the material of the novel. At bottom, the conflict of the later story is the conflict of faith versus works, even though the faith is a demonic one and the works are secular in character.

As his name suggests, Sheppard is a man desirous of being a pastor, though not of course in the conventional sense. For Christianity or any other system of religious belief he feels nothing but scorn. At the reformatory where he devotes his Saturdays to counseling wayward boys, he encounters his first prospective follower, Rufus Johnson—a wild, sullen, Satan-dominated grandson of a zealous "prophet." Rufus seems a compulsive criminal, and since he has a monstrous clubfoot, Sheppard immediately concludes that the boy's rebellion can be explained simply as compensation for feelings of inferiority. Sheppard also learns that Rufus has been brutally beaten by his grandfather and subjected to general neglect; therefore, when Rufus is paroled, Sheppard determines to befriend the boy, hoping to win his confidence and affection by giving him the "advantages" of a home and a loving parent.

As the story unfolds, the ambiguity of Sheppard's motives quickly becomes apparent. Not only does he consider himself a kind of surrogate priest, listening to the "confessions" of troubled teen-agers in a narrow, cramped office at the reformatory, but, having turned what he calls his unselfishness into a surrogate religion, he makes a fetish of self-denial, sleeping in "an ascetic-looking iron bed" in an uncarpeted room. For his work at the reformatory he receives no monetary compensation, and it is obvious that, in order for Sheppard to derive from it the psychic benefits he needs, his work must be done without pay. In this way he can maintain the fiction that he is "helping boys no one else care[s] about" and "receiving nothing" in return.

Driven as he is by the need to have continually before him an image of himself as "good" and unselfish, Sheppard is constantly annoyed by his son Norton, who hoards money and understands only one sense of sharing—his being given part of something that belongs to someone else. Sheppard contemplates with disgust the likelihood of Norton becoming a banker or, even worse, the manager of a loan company; and since Norton appears to be decidedly inferior to Rufus in intelligence, Sheppard virtually dismisses his son as an object worthy of his attention. Norton thereafter becomes a pawn in the struggle which develops between Sheppard and Rufus, once the delinquent accepts Sheppard's invitation to come and share their home.

The story's opening scene unveils Sheppard's confused attitudes toward the two boys. As the father sits eating breakfast cereal "mechanically," Norton wanders about the kitchen in search of a breakfast of his own—stale cake spread with peanut butter and ketchup. Sheppard lectures the boy on Rufus's pitiable condition (his mother is in the penitentiary and he must search for food in garbage cans) and suggests to Norton that he share his hoarded wealth with the delinquent, perhaps buying him a new shoe for his clubfoot. The boy is threatened, becomes agitated, and vomits—"a limp sweet batter" (148). Sheppard is overcome by a sense of the injustice of things—the intelligent Rufus "deprived of everything from birth" and the uninspiring "average or below average" Norton who "had had every advantage" (148). Of course, far from having had every advantage, Norton is utterly starved for love, love which Sheppard is incapable of giving him for two distinct but related reasons. First, Sheppard's need to be good and unselfish is so obsessive that it can only be satisfied when he helps those who have no right to expect his help. Given his psychological make-up, Sheppard is inevitably blind to the needs of those closest to him; he neglects Norton, because his desire to be "good" springs from an emptiness in himself which can only be filled by gratuitous deeds of charity in behalf of the world's suffering and underprivileged. His son Norton has a claim upon him, and hence no particular "merit" attaches to anything he may do for the boy. Thus he feels deep sympathy for Rufus who must scavenge for his food, but none at all for his own child who must make a breakfast of ketchup and stale cake. He laments the fate of a boy whose mother is in the penitentiary, but is without pity for his own son's longing for his dead mother. He is sensitive to the psychological scarring which he imagines Johnson's clubfoot has caused, while oblivious to the desperate loneliness of Norton.

The second reason for Sheppard's failure as a father is that, treating the human and the intellectual as interchangeable quantities, he imposes upon the living reality of his child an abstract image; then he responds to the image he has created rather than to the actual boy. Norton *is* selfish and he is (or appears to be) dull. But he is dull largely because of Sheppard's refusal to treat him as a significant human being. (It is important to note that Rufus awakens much that is repressed in Norton, who seems brighter, livelier toward the story's end; even Sheppard, myopic as he is, discovers in Norton's eyes an alertness which he had not noticed before [183].)

As he fails to see Norton except as a creation of his mind, so also does Sheppard refuse to see the real Rufus. The flesh and blood Rufus tells him that he commits crimes because he's "good at it," but Sheppard insists upon interpreting the boy's behavior according to textbook psychology. Rufus declares that he is in Satan's power, but because his intellectual system has made no provision for the demonic, Sheppard must reject this notion with an outraged cry of " 'Rubbish!' " (151). And, when Rufus speaks of heaven and hell as real places to which people go in an afterlife, Sheppard responds by assuring Rufus that he considers him "too intelligent" to believe such nonsense. Because Sheppard has attempted to force reality to conform to an intellectual construct of his own creation, intelligence is for him the decisive factor of human existence. Therefore, Rufus is a more "interesting" specimen of humanity than Norton.

It is his inordinate faith in reason which prevents Sheppard from understanding the power of feeling. He knows, of course, that Rufus possesses feelings of aggression; but because of his *idée fixe* that the source of these feelings is the clubfoot, Sheppard is incapable of taking seriously the boy's outrage at his self-righteousness and his propensity for playing God. Most importantly, Sheppard's obtuseness extends to his own feelings and to the motivation for his behavior. Convinced as he is that he is "good" and that he is " 'stronger than [Rufus]' " (180), Sheppard is shocked when he discovers that he can hate and is utterly confounded by the realization that, before the determined lucidity of Rufus's vision of damnation-with-the-possibility-of-salvation, his own self-serving "goodness" is as fragile as a paper doll's house.

The depth of Sheppard's confusion about his own feelings is revealed in the first episode involving Rufus and the police. Just prior to the arrival of the officers who come to arrest Rufus for a "smash job," Sheppard discovers the boy's absence and decides that his method of dealing with his protégé has been less successful than he had anticipated: "He had been over-lenient, too concerned to have Johnson like him. He felt a twinge of guilt." For a moment Sheppard determines to lay down strict rules for Rufus. But when he realizes that Rufus's response will be merely another assertion of independence and a threat to walk out, Sheppard panics: "Oh my God, he thought. He could not bring it to that. He would have to be firm but not make an issue of it" (167–68). Sheppard obviously is much "too concerned to have Johnson like him" to force the unambiguous understanding which the boy might respect. Yet the twinge of guilt is sufficient to cause Sheppard to fail Rufus at the one point in the story when the boy's confidence might have been won. As the police prepare to take Rufus off to jail, the boy denies knowledge of the crime and turns to his benefactor and protector and asks, "You believe me, don't you?"

> There was an appeal in his voice that Sheppard had not heard there before.
> This was crucial. The boy would have to learn that he could not be protected when he was guilty. "You'll have to go with him, Rufus," he said.

"You're going to let him take me and I tell you I ain't done a thing?" Johnson said shrilly.

Sheppard's face became harder as his sense of injury grew. The boy had failed him even before he had had a chance to give him the shoe. They were to have got it tomorrow. *All his regret turned suddenly on the shoe; his irritation at the sight of Johnson doubled* [emphasis added]. (P. 169)

Rufus *is* guilty, and, as we subsequently learn, he wants Sheppard to vouch for him so that he can ultimately compromise and expose this man who is determined to "save" him. The significance of this episode should not be underestimated, since it renders unmistakably clear that weakness in Sheppard which makes him an easy prey for Johnson's malice: Sheppard is so completely a captive of his confused feelings and his voracious hunger for ego satisfaction that he is incapable of dealing with any situation except in terms of its capacity to minister to his psychological needs. Thus, out of shame, he abdicates the little authority he has heretofore maintained over the boy, when he learns the following day that the police have arrested someone else for the crime and are releasing Rufus. Later, when Johnson rejects the new shoe with the scornful comment, " 'I don't need no new shoe. . . .' 'And when I do, I got ways of getting my own,' " Sheppard's response to this new rebuff confirms our image of him as a man totally incapable of responding to life except on the level of childish demands for ego gratification and equally childish petulance when those demands are frustrated.

He wanted to recover his good humor, *but every time he thought of the rejected shoe, he felt a new charge of irritation.* He did not trust himself even to look at Johnson. He realized that the boy had refused the shoe because he was insecure. Johnson had been frightened by his own gratitude. . . . *Grudgingly, Sheppard felt a*

slight return of sympathy for the boy. In a few minutes,
he lowered his paper and looked at him [emphases
added]. (P. 177)

Here by skillfully interweaving Sheppard's attempted
analysis of Johnson's psychological problems and intimations of Sheppard's failure to see his own psychological shortcomings as equally damaging, Flannery
O'Connor underscores this mock-pastor's moral and spiritual blindness. In Sheppard, Miss O'Connor has created
a classic example of one form of "bad faith" as defined
in existentialist philosophy—the detached observer or
manipulator who refuses to acknowledge that he is part
of the problem he is trying to analyze.

Because he treats the boy with a condescension rooted
in nothing more substantial than his limitless faith in
reason, Sheppard's image of himself is destined to be
shaken to its very foundations when he discovers the
implacable reality of Johnson's dedication to evil. Like
many of Miss O'Connor's earlier protagonists, both
among the positivists and the positive thinkers, Sheppard commits the fatal error of supposing that good and
evil are only words, denoting alternative conditioned responses to social reality. From this it follows that he
should assume that it is intelligence which can free man
(Rufus) from "evil" responses, just as he believes that
he himself is too intelligent to be evil. Hence, because
he considers Rufus endowed with intelligence equal to
his own, he persists in maintaining—in the face of
mounting evidence to the contrary—that the boy is "too
intelligent" to commit the crimes which the police at-
tribute to him. Only at the last, when Rufus has confessed to being the culprit, has allowed himself to be
caught, and has (falsely) accused Sheppard of making
"[i]morr'l suggestions"—only then does Sheppard recognize the impotence of his philosophy that man can make

of himself anything he wishes, by virtue of intellect alone.

In one respect, Sheppard is correct about Rufus; the boy *is* intelligent, so much so, in fact, that he immediately perceives that Sheppard's supposedly humanitarian interest in others is in reality a form of self-aggrandizement (cf. Julian of "Everything That Rises"). Therefore, Rufus insists upon being what he is, rather than a creature of Sheppard's theories. He is obstinate, vindictive, malicious, ungrateful, unregenerate—all these and more. In him we encounter once again the criminal-compulsive who so often serves as a spokesman for the author's most deeply felt convictions. Like that earlier prototype, The Misfit, Rufus declares that man faces a choice between Jesus and the devil; but Rufus's faith in both the divine and the satanic is less anxiety-ridden, more rooted in positive conviction. He revels in his depravity while at the same time maintaining that " '[n]obody can save [him] but Jesus' " (180) and that if and when he does repent, he is going " 'to be a preacher,' " because " 'If you're going to do it, it's no sense in doing it halfway' " (183). Here Rufus sounds very much like Tarwater, whom he resembles in other respects, principally, I think, in the clarity of his understanding of the relation of act and consequence and in his unswerving insistence upon the primacy of will over reason.

Near the story's conclusion, as Johnson is about to be taken off to jail, he shouts: " 'I lie and steal because I'm good at it! My foot don't have a thing to do with it! The lame shall enter first! The halt'll be gathered together. When I get ready to be saved, Jesus'll save me, not that lying stinking atheist' " (188–89). This outburst causes Sheppard to reflect: " 'I have nothing to reproach myself with' " (189). Then, as he counts over his "selfless" acts of devotion to the cause of "sav[ing]

Johnson for some decent kind of service," there reverberates through his mind, like the drumbeat of an attacking enemy force, the words, " 'I did more for him than I did for my own child' " (189). Immediately, in a crescendo of revelation, Sheppard hears the "jubilant voice" of Rufus shouting, " 'Satan has you in his power,' " and at that moment, in the boy's mocking eyes, Sheppard sees an image of "the clear-eyed Devil," malicious and triumphant (189).

> Norton's face rose before him, empty, forlorn. . . . His heart constricted with a repulsion for himself so clear and intense that he gasped for breath. He had stuffed his own emptiness with good works like a glutton. He had ignored his own child to feed his vision of himself. . . . His image of himself shrivelled until everything was black before him. He sat there paralyzed, aghast. (P. 190)

At this instant, Sheppard experiences a wave of "agonizing love" for his son, only to discover the boy hanging from a rafter in the attic where "he had launched his flight into space" (190).

Sheppard's failure as a human being is figured here with exquisite irony, since it had been his ambition that his son become an astronaut, conquering space and exploring the stars. But Norton has responded instead to Rufus's very concrete, vivid and immediate faith in heaven and hell, remaining impervious to Sheppard's lectures about the glories of science and man's penetration of the darkness of the universe. Affirming his own humanity, Norton chooses to join his mother, whom he believes he has sighted in heaven (through the telescope Sheppard had bought principally to interest Rufus in science!), in preference to continuing his empty existence with the man who has given him "every advantage." It is Sheppard who at last begins to penetrate the darkness, not of outer space but of his own heart. Perhaps Sheppard is too much of a caricature to be fully believable; [10] and perhaps for this reason he cannot be considered a tragic figure. Yet this story has about it an ironic fatality as beautifully contrived and as inexorable as that of any Greek tragedy.

Not the least of the virtues of this tale is the clarity with which Flannery O'Connor has portrayed the manner in which a passionate belief in the truth of the divine Word may exist *simultaneously* with a passionate commitment to the demonic principle. (Rufus swallows a page from the Bible and cries, " 'I've eaten it like Ezekiel and it was honey to my mouth!' " [185]. On the other hand, the success of his lying and stealing is a source of immense satisfaction to him, and he assumes the role of Satan's helper with a gusto which is breathtaking.) Rufus has been described as "a basic figure in modern existentialist literature—the criminal who is seeking God," and has been compared to Dostoevsky's Raskolnikov. [11] The comparison is in many respects apt, not so much because of a resemblance uniting the two characters as such, but because of the basic similarity of the religious or metaphysical questions explored in *Crime and Punishment* and in Flannery O'Connor's novella. Rufus's clubfoot clearly symbolizes a crisis of the spirit not unlike that by which Dostoevsky's hero is afflicted, and the experiences of both Raskolnikov and Rufus suggest that at certain stages in the disintegration of a spiritual tradition, it is only through apparent dedication to the devil and through motiveless crime that a new, authentic humanity can be born. [12]

This notion of commitment to the satanic principle illumines certain features of Miss O'Connor's work that have long been problematic. That the devil plays a conspicuous role in her fiction there is no denying, and one sympathetic commentator has suggested that Flannery O'Connor's authorial voice and that of her devil often appear indistinguishable. From this observation John Hawkes concluded that, whether she was conscious of it or not, "as writer [Flannery O'Connor] was on the devil's side." [13] Granting the truth of Hawkes's description of her authorial stance as sometimes "black," and of the creative impulse in her writing as often "so unflagging and so unpredictable as to become, in a sense, 'immoral,' " [14] I believe Miss O'Connor's attraction to the demonic can better be explained as part of that metaphysical enterprise mentioned in Chapter One— the quest of being and the Holy. For it appears to have been one of her cardinal beliefs that without a recovery of the demonic there could be no true "rediscovery of man." As we have seen in our examination of such characters as Mrs. Cope, the grandmother, and Sheppard, O'Connor's fiction projects an image of man who has lost so completely his capacity for apprehending true evil that he is equally incapable of recognizing true good. And his addiction to superficial and platitudinous conceptions of both good and evil seems the consequence of a loss even more profound—the experience of the self as grounded in being.

Both O'Connor's positivists and her positive thinkers, then, like the "faithless pilgrims" of Conrad's *Heart of Darkness*, suffer from a malaise which is, at bottom, ontological. Dispossessed both of their original innocence and of their postlapsarian knowledge, they seek, however unconsciously, a way back into being. But the way to being is fraught with peril, since it entails confronting the irrational and destructive aspects of the self, facing up to the ugliness and cruelty of life, exploring that foul "dungeon of the heart," which Hawthorne, Dostoevsky and other spiritual forefathers of Flannery O'Connor considered of the essence of human existence but which centuries of moralistic Christianity and bourgeois culture have tended to deny or obscure.

Thus when Flannery O'Connor set out to represent "the conflict between an attraction for the Holy and the disbelief in it which we breathe in with the air of the times," she in fact created a body of fiction one of whose major accomplishments is to present a persuasive dramatic case for the reality of the demonic. But belief in the demonic is only one step from belief in the Holy, for the two stand, so Paul Tillich has argued, in dialectical relation to each other. ("The divine," Tillich states, "embraces itself and the demonic," and he talks of "divine holiness" and "demonic holiness.") [15] Flannery O'Connor's intention, apparently, was to render intelligible the concept of demonic holiness as a way of affirming the reality of holiness itself, and in so doing to bear witness to some depth reality, some "ground of Being" (to borrow another phrase from Tillich), where both the demonic and the Holy reside and out of which man's own being emerges.[16]

Flannery O'Connor, it might finally be argued, sought to recover the depth dimension of existence in order to adumbrate an answer to the "ontological void" posited by Ionesco and other contemporary artists and philosophers. But she recognized that the recovery of depth, or being, was possible only by stripping the masks from men whose fraudulent righteousness had rendered them too complacent even to be damned. Therefore her strategy as a writer was to make as vivid as possible the reality of the demonic, to celebrate, as it were, "spiritual crime," to employ the shock of evil over and over again, in the hope that, finally, by plunging into those fearful psychic depths she might bring up some evidence that, in a time marked by moral chaos and ontological deprivation, it was yet being, not absurdity, which would have the last word.

Notes

1 – The Background: Life, Works, and Reputation

1. Robert Fitzgerald, "Introduction," *Everything That Rises Must Converge* (New York: Farrar, Straus & Giroux, 1965), p. viii. While there are several reminiscences of Flannery O'Connor, there is as yet no biography and Fitzgerald's "Introduction" remains the most complete and reliable source of biographical information.

2. "The King of the Birds," in Flannery O'Connor, *Mystery and Manners: Occasional Prose*, p. 4.

3. Fitzgerald, p. xii.

4. Ibid., p. xxi.

5. Richard Stern, "Flannery O'Connor" A Remembrance and Some Letters," *Shenandoah*, 16 (Winter 1965), 5–10.

6. Sr. Kathleen Feeley, *Flannery O'Connor: Voice of the Peacock.*

7. Review of *The Phenomenon of Man, American Scholar* (Fall 1961), 618.

8. O'Connor, *Mystery and Manners*, p. 197.

9. Ibid., p. 203.

10. Ibid., p. 206.

11. Ibid., p. 159.

12. Ibid.

13. Ibid., p. 160.

14. Theodore Solotaroff, "You *Can* Go Home Again," *New York Herald Tribune's Book Week*, 30 May 1965, p. 13.

15. Warren Coffey, "Flannery O'Connor," *Commentary* (November 1965), 94.

16. "John Hawkes: An Interview," *Wisconsin Studies in Contemporary Literature* (Summer 1965), 143–44.

17. Quoted in John Hawkes, "Flannery O'Connor's Devil," 397.

18. O'Connor, *Mystery and Manners*, pp. 33–34.

19. Quoted in Ihab Hassan, *Radical Innocence: Studies in the Contemporary American Novel* (Princeton: Princeton University Press, 1961), p. 26.

20. Quoted in Josephine Hendin, *The World of Flannery O'Connor*, p. 18.

21. David Eggenschwiler, *The Christian Humanism of Flannery O'Connor*, pp. 16, 17.

22. Ibid., p. 32.

23. Miles Orvell, *Invisible Parade: The Fiction of Flannery O'Connor*, p. 27.

24. Ibid., p. 24.

25. Stanley Hyman, *Flannery O'Connor*, p. 37.

26. Hendin. See especially Chapter 1.

27. Prefatory note to 2nd edition of *Wise Blood*, included in Flannery O'Connor, *Three by Flannery O'Connor*.

2—Wise Blood

1. Flannery O'Connor, *Mystery and Manners: Occasional Prose*, p. 153.

2. *Wise Blood*, in Flannery O'Connor, *Three by Flannery O'Connor*, p. 90. Also included in this edition are *A Good Man Is Hard to Find* and *The Violent Bear It Away*. Subsequent references to these works are to this edition.

3. Jonathan Baumbach, *The Landscape of Nightmare*, p. 92.

4. Miles Orvell, *Invisible Parade: The Fiction of Flannery O'Connor*, p. 86.

5. See especially Stuart L. Burns, "The Evolution of *Wise Blood*," *Modern Fiction Studies*, 16 (Summer 1970), 157–58.

6. David Eggenschwiler, *The Christian Humanism of Flannery O'Connor*, pp. 104–7.

7. "Revelation," in *Everything That Rises Must Converge*, p. 206.

8. Albert Camus, *The Rebel* (New York: Vintage Books, 1965), p. 24.

9. Eggenschwiler, pp. 112–14.

10. O'Connor, *Mystery and Manners*, p. 185.

11. Ibid., p. 83.

3—A Good Man Is Hard to Find

1. Robert Fitzgerald, "Introduction," *Everything That Rises Must Converge* (New York: Farrar, Straus & Giroux, 1965), p. xxii.

2. Stanley Hyman, *Flannery O'Connor*, p. 17.
3. O'Connor, *Mystery and Manners*, p. 111.
4. V. V. Zenkovsky, "Dostoevsky's Religious and Philosophical Views," in *Dostoevsky*, Twentieth Century Views, ed. René Wellek (Englewood Cliffs, N.J.: Prentice, 1962), p. 136.
5. Hyman, p. 36.
6. Ibid., p. 16.
7. For a detailed discussion of the multiple significance of the plaster statue, see Richard Coleman, "Flannery O'Connor: A Scrutiny of Two Forms of Her Many-Leveled Art," *Phoenix* (1966), 55.
8. O'Connor, *Mystery and Manners*, p. 175.
9. Leon V. Driskell and Joan T. Brittain, *The Eternal Crossroads: The Art of Flannery O'Connor*, pp. 59–80.
10. O'Connor, *Mystery and Manners*, p. 157.

4—The Violent Bear It Away

1. Robert Fitzgerald, "Introduction," *Everything That Rises Must Converge* (New York: Farrar, Straus & Giroux, 1965), p. xxi.
2. Stanley Hyman, *Flannery O'Connor*, p. 24.
3. O'Connor, *Mystery and Manners*, p. 179.
4. Hyman, p. 24.
5. Ibid., p. 25.
6. O'Connor, *The Violent Bear It Away*, p. 357.
7. Francis Fergusson, *The Idea of a Theater* (Garden City, N.Y.: Doubleday, 1953; originally published by Princeton University Press, 1949), p. 174.
8. Robert O. Bowen, "Hope vs. Despair in the New Gothic Novel," *Renascence* (Spring 1961), 147–52.
9. Thomas M. Lorch, "Flannery O'Connor: A Christian Allegorist," *Critique*, 10 (1968), 77.
10. Prefatory note to the 1962 edition of *Wise Blood*, in Flannery O'Connor, *Three by Flannery O'Connor*.
11. Lorch, p. 78.
12. O'Connor, *Mystery and Manners*, pp. 33–34.
13. Quoted in Granville Hicks, "A Writer at Home with Her Heritage," *Saturday Review* (12 May 1962), 23.
14. "*The Violent Bear It Away*: A Study in Imagery," *Xavier University Studies* (Spring 1962), 194. Emphasis added.
15. J. Oates Smith, "Ritual and Violence in Flannery O'Connor," *Thought* (Winter 1966), 555.

16. Marion Montgomery, "The Sense of Violation: Notes toward a Definition of 'Southern' Fiction," *Georgia Review* (Fall 1965), 281.

17. Louis D. Rubin, Jr., "Flannery O'Connor and the Bible Belt," in *The Added Dimension: The Art and Mind of Flannery O'Connor*, eds. Melvin J. Friedman and Lewis A. Lawson, p. 63.

18. Ibid.

19. Ibid., p. 62.

20. Ibid., p. 64.

21. Ibid.

22. Ibid., p. 65.

23. Ibid., p. 66.

5—Everything That Rises Must Converge

1. Flannery O'Connor, *Everything That Rises Must Converge*, p. 23. Subsequent references are to this edition.

2. *The Future of Man*, pp. 72–73. Quoted in Leon V. Driskell and Joan T. Brittain, *The Eternal Crossroads: The Art of Flannery O'Connor*, p. 140.

3. Teilhard de Chardin, *The Phenomenon of Man* (New York: Harper & Row, 1961), p. 263.

4. Ibid.

5. Theodore Solotaroff, "You *Can* Go Home Again," New York *Herald Tribune's Book Week*, 30 May 1965, p. 13.

6. Ibid.

7. Hyman, *Flannery O'Connor*, p. 28.

8. Sr. Bernetta Quinn, O.S.F., "Flannery O'Connor, a Realist of Distances," in Friedman and Lawson, eds., *The Added Dimension*, p. 168.

9. Ibid.

10. See Hyman, p. 45.

11. Ted R. Spivey, "Flannery O'Connor's View of God and Man," p. 202.

12. Ibid.

13. John Hawkes, "Flannery O'Connor's Devil," p. 400.

14. Ibid., p. 399.

15. Paul Tillich, *Systematic Theology*, I, pp. 215–18.

16. For a more detailed discussion of the ontological implications of Flannery O'Connor's "demonic strategies," see Preston M. Browning, Jr., "Flannery O'Connor and the Demonic," *Modern Fiction Studies*, 19 (Spring 1973), 29–41.

Selected Bibliography

Baumbach, Jonathan. *The Landscape of Nightmare*. New York: New York University Press, 1965.

Browning, Preston M., Jr. " 'Parker's Back': Flannery O'Connor's Iconography of Salvation by Profanity," *Studies in Short Fiction* 6 (Fall 1969), 525–35.

———. "Flannery O'Connor and the Demonic," *Modern Fiction Studies* 19 (Spring 1973), 29–41.

Burns, Stuart L. "Flannery O'Connor's *The Violent Bear It Away*: Apotheosis in Failure." *Sewanee Review* 76 (Spring 1968), 319–36.

Driskell, Leon V. and Joan T. Brittain. *The Eternal Crossroads: The Art of Flannery O'Connor*. Lexington: University of Kentucky Press, 1971.

Eggenschwiler, David. *The Christian Humanism of Flannery O'Connor*. Detroit: Wayne State University Press, 1972.

Feeley, Sr. Kathleen. *Flannery O'Connor: Voice of the Peacock*. New Brunswick, N.J.: Rutgers University Press, 1972.

Friedman, Melvin J. and Lewis A. Lawson, eds., *The Added Dimension: the Art and Mind of Flannery O'Connor*. New York: Fordham University Press, 1966.

Hawkes, John. "Flannery O'Connor's Devil," *Sewanee Review* 70 (Summer 1962), 395–407.

Hendin, Josephine. *The World of Flannery O'Connor*. Bloomington: Indiana University Press, 1970.

Hyman, Stanley Edgar. *Flannery O'Connor*. University of Minnesota Pamphlets on American Writers, no. 54. Minneapolis: University of Minnesota Press, 1966.

Lorch, Thomas M. "Flannery O'Connor: a Christian Allegorist," *Critique* 10 (1968), 69–80.

Malin, Irving. *New American Gothic*. Carbondale: Southern Illinois University Press, 1962.

Martin, Carter W. *The True Country: Themes in the Fiction*

of Flannery O'Connor. Nashville: Vanderbilt University Press, 1969.

Montgomery, Marion. "The Sense of Violation: Notes Toward a Definition of 'Southern Fiction.'" *Georgia Review* 19 (Fall 1965), 278–87.

Muller, Gilbert H. *Nightmares and Visions: Flannery O'Connor and the Catholic Grotesque.* Athens: University of Georgia Press, 1972.

O'Connor, Flannery. *The Complete Stories.* New York: Farrar, Straus & Giroux, 1971.

———. *Everything That Rises Must Converge.* New York: Farrar, Straus & Giroux, 1965.

———. *A Good Man Is Hard to Find and Other Stories.* New York: Harcourt, Brace & Co., 1955.

———. *Mystery and Manners: Occasional Prose.* Eds. Sally and Robert Fitzgerald, New York: Farrar, Straus & Giroux, 1969.

———. *The Violent Bear It Away.* New York: Farrar, Straus & Cudahy, 1960.

———. *Three By Flannery O'Connor.* New York: Signet Books, 1964.

———. "Why Do the Heathen Rage?" *Esquire.* (July 1963), 60–61.

———. *Wise Blood.* 2d ed. With an Introduction by the author. New York: Farrar, Straus & Cudahy, 1962.

Orvell, Miles. *Invisible Parade: the Fiction of Flannery O'Connor.* Philadelphia: Temple University Press, 1972.

Smith, J. Oates. "Ritual and Violence in Flannery O'Connor," *Thought* 41 (Winter 1966), 545–60.

Spivey, Ted R. "Flannery O'Connor's View of God and Man," *Studies in Short Fiction* 1 (Spring 1964), 200–206.

Tillich, Paul. *Systematic Theology* I. Chicago: University of Chicago Press, 1951.

Index

Abnormality: interest in, 2, 44, 45, 46, 108–9. *See also* Grotesqueness

Absalom, Absalom!, 102–3

Absurd: acceptance of, 35–36

Alienation, 41, 70

Alter ego. *See* Self: reflection of

Ambivalence, 34, 74–76, 79, 81, 88–89, 101, 102–5, 126. *See also* Choice

Andalusia, 4, 9

Animality, 25, 29–30

Antagonists: relationship with protagonists, 17

Aquinas, Saint Thomas, 6

Art: O'Connor's interest in, 2–3

"Artificial Nigger, The," 60–69, 71, 100

Augustine, Saint, 6

Bailey, 54–55

Baptism; of Bishop Rayber, 75, 79, 82, 83, 89, 92; mentioned, 77

Baudelaire, Charles, 21

Being: quest for, 13–14, 129–30

Bible: Southerners' knowledge of, 8

Blasphemy, 26, 27, 30, 32, 35, 36, 74

Blindness: spiritual, 25–26, 70; of Hazel Motes, 26, 36–37; of Asa Hawks, 30–32

Bowen, Robert, 87

Boyd, Powell, 52–53

Brittain, Joan T., 69

Buber, Martin, 6

Buford, 84

Burns, Stuart L., 74

Camus, Albert, 9, 21, 35

Capote, Truman, 11

Carlyle, Thomas, 21

Catholicism, 7–9, 38, 85, 89

"Catholic Novelists and Their Readers," 38

Characters: types of, 15–18, 41, 42, 50–51, 57, 108; conflict between, 17; motivation of, 26; O'Connor's handling of, 26, 40; female, 59

Chase, Richard, 6

Chestny, Julian, 100–108, 126

Chestny, Mrs., 100–107

Childhood: desire for, 47, 49, 50; influences of, 88–89, 92

Choice: theme of, 21, 22, 24, 25, 35, 74–76, 86–89, 126. *See also* Ambivalence; Freedom

Christ. *See* God; Jesus

137

Appendix

"Parker's Back": Flannery O'Connor's Iconography of Salvation by Profanity

As Flannery O'Connor on several occasions observed, one of the major difficulties encountered by the artist with Christian concerns in a radically secular age is the embodiment of his vision in artistic form in such a manner as neither to vitiate the vision nor to violate the form. And, as a chorus of critics has recently testified, Miss O'Connor seemed more often than not to have performed this arduous task. Without watering down her Christian convictions, she was yet able in a considerable number of instances to fashion tales that possess the inner logic, the autonomy, the self-sustaining tension of genuine art while at the save time serving as "vehicles" for those convictions. Occasionally, as in "The Enduring Chill," she failed; or, rather, almost succeeded, for, if we except the overly explicit and too-often-repeated symbolism of the Holy Spirit, this story achieves a perfection of its own, in the use of irony as brilliant as any in the entire O'Connor corpus. Usually, however, an O'Connor story is an expertly constructed house in which narrative progression and naturalistic detail cohabit with spiritual vision on amicable terms, neither trying to relegate the other (like a poor country cousin) to the dark limbo of the basement apartment. To be sure, Flannery O'Connor spoke of herself without apologies as a Christian writer, but good Southerner that she was, she loved to tell a story for its own sake; and good craftsman that she was, knew that it was useless to embody a "message" in a story that could not stand scrutiny as a piece of honest fiction. The current critical interest in her work, increasing as it does at a startling pace, is perhaps an index to the success with which she maintained this precarious balance upon which a well-ordered and harmonious "house of fiction" rests.

With this interest in mind, I shall examine what Brainard Cheney calls "the characteristic dramatic strategy of her short stories." Flannery O'Connor begins, Cheney says,

> . . . with familiar surfaces, in an action that seems secular at the outset, and in a secular tone of satire or humor. Before you know it, the naturalistic situation has become metaphysical, and the action appropriate to it comes with a surprise, an unaccountability that is humorous, grimly humorous, however shocking.[1]

Nowhere, I think, does Miss O'Connor use this strategy more effectively and with more unexpected results than in "Parker's Back." Here the "natural" does indeed shade off into the "metaphysical"; though it might be more accurate to say they occupy the same space, the metaphysical not so much supplanting the natural as gradually manifesting itself through the secular and the natural.

What seems to me especially striking about this story is that in it Miss O'Connor has used the most unlikely expression of contemporary secularism—tattooing—as a kind of analogue for that sense of the Other, with its attendant feelings of awe, fascination and dread, which Rudolf Otto defined as the experience of the "numinous." And this, surely, is the subject of the story: the awakening to the awe-ful presence of the numinous (the Holy) in one who had beforehand been as insensitive as a stone, "as ordinary as a loaf of bread."² At the same time it is the study of an individual who is subconsciously searching for an identity that is his all the while and which he is able to accept only after a series of encounters with a Power fully invested with the characteristics of the numinous. The skillful interweaving of the two motifs makes this one of Flannery O'Connor's most arresting and, to my mind, most mature stories.

Miss O'Connor's protagonist is a youth named O. E. (Obadiah Elihue) Parker, who at fourteen visits a county fair where he beholds a veritable walking tattoo, a man covered by an "arabesque of men and beasts and flowers" (223). Parker, whose habitually gaping mouth symbolizes mental and spiritual emptiness, at this moment experiences an exaltation of the spirit such as would normally be associated with religious or patriotic dedication. For the reader at any rate, Parker's response has overtones of a classic religious conversion, although the meaning of the event is, from the boy's point of view, kept appropriately undifferentiated.

> Parker had never before felt the least motion of wonder in himself. Until he saw the man at the fair, it did not enter his head that there was anything out of the ordinary about the fact that he existed. Even then it did not enter his head, but a peculiar unease settled in him. It was as if a blind boy had been turned so gently in a different direction that he did not know his destination had been changed. (*ibid.*)

It is clear, I believe, that Parker's "unease" is the outgrowth of his failure to establish in youth and early manhood a unifying and sustaining identity. The single experience that has marked his life as "different" is the encounter with the man at the fair; but Parker's attempted identification with the tat-

tooed man is thwarted because, no matter how many tattoos
he acquires (and over a period of years he acquires a prodi-
gious number), he is never able to achieve that perfect "arabesque" of colors which was the occasion of his "awakening."
Each new tattoo leads to further dissatisfaction as its fascination wears off and as a meaningful pattern, the ultimate object
of Parker's half-conscious longing, fails to materialize. In this
respect a prototype of modern man, Parker derives his (tran-
sient) sense of identity from external properties acquired at
random, things that by their very nature cannot produce a
pattern, will not cohere.[3]

Parker's "unease" leads him into various jobs of short du-
ration, into a five-year hitch in the Navy, which concludes
with nine months in the brig and a dishonorable discharge,
and finally into marriage to a homely, dried-up country girl
named Sarah Ruth Cates. The daughter of a fundamentalist
preacher, Sarah Ruth is the antithesis of everything Parker
thinks admirable: she neither smokes, drinks, nor swears;
considers his tattoos an abomination; and, when he suggests
that they lie down together in the back of his truck, knocks
him completely off his seat and onto the ground. Already
baffled by his own behavior since from the very beginning
he had thought her too ugly to look at twice, Parker makes
"up his mind then and there to have nothing further to do
with her" (229). Yet the following sentence reads: "They were
married in the County Ordinary's office because Sarah Ruth
thought churches were idolatrous." Why, the reader may be
inclined to ask, should Parker, who had promised himself
never to be "caught" by a woman, marry—of all possible
choices—this girl, so fanatically pietistic, so strange, so radically different from the others he has known. The question, I
would suggest, implies its own answer, for it is precisely her
difference, her strangeness, her "mysteriousness" (not unlike

that of the tattooed man) that takes hold of Parker, making him act in uncanny, inexplicable ways.

One can locate a further explanation of Parker's choice of a wife in the hidden powers of his name, a power that, like the name itself, is biblical in implication. About his given name, Obadiah Elihue, Parker feels an irrepressible shame, and, until he meets Sarah Ruth, he guards with irrational ferocity the secret the initials "O. E." hide. Therefore, when Sarah Ruth cajoles him into revealing this secret, a subtle bond is established between them. Though it is not clear that Parker understands the religious significance of his name, Sarah Ruth receives it "as a sign," immediately recognizing all of its prophetic overtones. (In the Old Testament Obadiah was a sixth-century prophet who, in a "vision," predicted the destruction that would befall Edom for her unrighteousness; while Elihue figures in the Job story, not as one of the "comforters," but as a younger man who rebukes Job for his presumption, reminding him of the unknowable [and apparently ambiguous] ways of God: "God is greater than man. . . . God speaks in one way, and in two, though man does not perceive it. In a dream, in a vision of the night, when deep sleep falls upon men, then he opens the ears of men, and terrifies them with warnings, that he may turn man aside from his deed, and cut off pride from man" [Job, 33:12–18]). Having been endowed with these portentous names, Parker comes to Sarah Ruth as a kind of emissary from God, and thus we might say that it is *she* who chooses *him*, Parker merely submitting, in this instance, as in others, to "whatever instinct of this kind [that came] to him" (241).

Whatever her motives may be, Parker, of course, thinks he can explain Sarah Ruth:

> Sometimes he supposed that she had married him
> because she meant to save him. At other times he

had a suspicion that she actually liked everything she
said she didn't. He could account for her one way or
another ... (220).

What he *knows* he cannot explain is himself: "it was himself he
could not understand." Parker's failure to understand himself
is, patently, a failure to understand the restlessness, the eternal
dissatisfaction that plagues him and for which Sarah Ruth,
with her strange, piercing "icepick" eyes and her uncompromising religious fervor, comes to stand as a kind of objective
correlative. Thus he marries her out of the same blind urging
that drives him back periodically to the tattoo artist, and with
identical results—the "unease" rages as violently as ever.

Marriage, in fact, exacerbates Parker's dissatisfaction, which
in time becomes so acute that he begins to lose weight and
develops a nervous tic, while his eyes take on "a hollow preoccupied expression" (232). Each morning he determines to
leave this wife who seems to derive no pleasure from anything
he says or does and who pesters him incessantly about his
poor chances before "the judgment seat of God." Each night
he returns, gloomier than before, more hopelessly ensnared
in a relationship that is morbidly fascinating at the same time
that it repels. Finally, inspiration comes to Parker: he will have
a tattoo drawn on his back (the rest of his body being already
covered), something "religious" that Sarah Ruth will find ir-
resistible. At this point the two things by which Parker has
sought relief from his haunting restlessness converge. This
will be *the* tattoo, a grand consummation of the "art" he has
acquired over the years; it will be, as well, a means of appeas-
ing and thus silencing, once and for all, Sarah Ruth and her
"sharp tongue." If he can "get exactly the right one to bring
Sarah Ruth to heel" (231–32), Parker speculates, his troubles
will be over.

But like all of Flannery O'Connor's protagonists who believe that they can control their destinies by some kind of manipulation of themselves or others, Parker is soon to discover that he is, in truth, "a blind boy . . . turned . . . in a different direction," though on this occasion the turning is singularly ungentle. For several days later, while baling hay in a field with a large tree at its center, Parker is so preoccupied with the problem of the "right" tattoo that he drives the tractor straight into the tree, setting both on fire. As Parker is catapulted through the air, he involuntarily shouts the words "GOD ABOVE"—an utterance the attentive reader of Flannery O'Connor will recognize as a "profanity" meant to suggest a subliminal acknowledgement of the sacred while losing none of its profane qualities. The passage describing this episode is so central to the action of the story that it warrants quotation in its entirety:

> He landed on his back while the tractor crashed up-
> sidedown into the tree and burst into flame. The first
> thing Parker saw were his shoes, quickly being eaten
> by the fire; one was caught under the tractor, the other
> was some distance away, burning all by itself. He was
> not in them. He could feel the hot breath of the burn-
> ing tree on his face. He scrambled backwards, still
> sitting, his eyes cavernous, and if he had known how
> to cross himself he would have done it. (232–33)

As Parker *backs away* from the tractor and then turns to run, barefooted, to his truck, twice falling to his knees, the significance of this event with all of its religious (especially Biblical) imagery, is immediately evident. Clearly, Parker's experience parallels that of Moses, and, deficient though he may be in intelligence, Parker "knows" that he is on holy ground. He knows, too, "that there [has] been a great change in his life, a leap forward into a worse unknown, and that there [is] nothing he [can] do about it. It [is] for all intents accomplished" (233).

And, so, in a sense, it is. For after this experience of the burning bush, everything Parker does has about it a predetermined character. Still shoeless, he rushes headlong to the city, bursts in upon his favorite tattoo artist demanding a picture of God for his back, and insists upon having the work begun that evening. As he leafs through the book the artist shows him (Miss O'Connor's mordant humor is nowhere more in evidence than when she has the artist inform Parker that the "up-to-date" pictures are toward the back), something tells him to return to the earlier sections. When Parker sees again the face of the "flat stern Byzantine Christ with all-demanding eyes," he knows infallibly that this is the tattoo he must have. Of course, he is right. Although he does not yet know it, it is himself who must be satisfied, not Sarah Ruth; and for that purpose the Byzantine Christ, from which a sense of the numinous streams forth, is the inevitable choice. In its "all-demanding eyes" Parker dimly perceives the "GOD ABOVE" whom he is fleeing and toward whom he is driven.

Throughout this story (as is true of many others by Flannery O'Connor), there is an emphasis upon eyes and upon seeing that is worth noting. Parker's eyes, while he is on duty with the Navy, are described as "reflect[ing] the immense spaces around him as if they were a microcosm of the mysterious sea" (335), a trope intended, perhaps, to suggest Parker's susceptibility to the elemental, nonrational, and demonic-holy powers in and above nature. In sharp contrast, Sarah Ruth's eyes have about them a piercing "icepick" quality, a quality that, like everything else associated with her, holds Parker with a perverse fascination. Not surprisingly, then, it is the eyes of the Christ to which Parker's attention is initially drawn; and when, after the preliminary sketching is done and he sees only a blank face, he feels cheated: "It don't have eyes," he complains. His attitude toward the eyes is predictably ambivalent, however; and while he attempts to sleep that night on a cot in a Gospel mission, his soul is haunted by their inexorable stare:

> He longed miserably for Sarah Ruth. Her sharp tongue and ice pick eyes were the only comfort he could bring to mind. He decided he was losing it. Her eyes appeared soft and dilatory compared with the eyes in the book, for even though he could not summon up the exact look of those eyes, he could still feel their penetration. He felt as though, under their gaze, he was as transparent as the wing of a fly. (237)

The following day, when the work is completed, Parker evinces a sullen unwillingness to face the image now indelibly inscribed on his back, and the artist must use force to get him into position between the mirrors. "Parker looked, turned white and moved away. The eyes in the reflected face continued to look at him—still, straight, all-demanding, enclosed in silence" (239).

Reluctant prophet that he is, Parker makes one final attempt to escape his destiny. He drinks a pint of whisky as if he were gulping a glass of water and then goes to a pool hall he has patronized from time to time, there provoking a wild mêlée after news of his tattoo spreads and he is taunted about having "gone and got religion." That the calm of the pool hall, after his violent ejection, should be declared to be "as nerve shattering as if the . . . room were the ship from which Jonah had been cast into the sea" (241), adds one more Biblical echo to Parker's story and prepares us for the spiritual crisis that immediately follows. Like Jonah after his travail in the belly of the whale, Parker sits on the ground "examining his soul."

He saw it as a spider web of facts and lies that was not at all important to him but which appeared to be necessary in spite of his opinion. *The eyes that were now forever on his back were eyes to be obeyed.* He was as certain of it as he had ever been of anything. Throughout his life, grumbling and sometimes cursing, often afraid, once in rapture, Parker had obeyed whatever instinct of this kind had come to him—in rapture when his spirit lifted at the sight of the tattooed man at the fair, afraid when he had joined the navy, grumbling when he had married Sarah Ruth.

The thought of her brought him slowly to his feet. She would know what he had to do. She would clear up the rest of it, and she would at least be pleased. It seemed to him that, all along, that was what he wanted, to please her. . . . His head was almost clear of liquor and he observed that his dissatisfaction was gone, but he felt not quite like himself. *It was as if he were himself but a stranger to himself,* driving into a new country though everything he saw was familiar to him, even at night. (241, emphasis added)

The language of this passage makes possible only one interpretation: Parker has at last accepted the imperative implied in his name and manifested to him in the burning bush episode and in the eyes of the Byzantine Christ. Though his particular mission in life is still unclear, there is no longer any doubt that he is one of the Lord's chosen, called to be the bearer of the Word (literally, the image) of God amidst an unbelieving people. He is Moses and Jonah and Obadiah and O. E. Parker; he has, finally, an identity that he can no longer evade and that he finds at once strange and familiar, unanticipated and inevitable. He's through running, through seeking; all that remains is for Sarah Ruth to reveal the meaning of his election, the specific purpose of his "call."

But Parker's life, which has been full of queer, unaccountable happenings, has one more hidden turning awaiting him. For when he arrives home in the pre-dawn gloom, he finds a locked door that Sarah Ruth refuses to open until he acknowledges his proper, biblical name. Each time he knocks, "the same unfeeling voice" asks, "Who's there?" and each time his "Me,"—"O. E." is met with chilling silence. Then, in a moment of near-mystical communion, Parker turns his head "as if he expected someone behind him to give him the answer" and sees in the first streaks of dawn "a tree of light burst[ing] over the skyline" (242). Parker is transfixed and when the voice inside asks once more, in a tone absolute and final, "Who's there . . . ?" Parker himself now has the answer.

> Parker bent down and put his mouth near the stuffed keyhole. "Obadiah," he whispered and all at once he felt the light pouring through him, turning his spider web soul into a perfect arabesque of colors, a garden of trees and birds and beasts.
> "Obadiah Elihue!" he whispered. (243)

In this scene all of the motifs of the story coalesce. The tree of light or fire (the numinous) permeates Parker's soul at that moment when he is able to acknowledge his real name; his identity is confirmed as the perfect arabesque that he had sought for his body but never found (the illusion of identity established via externals) is seen instead as a vision of the spirit. The spider web image, suggestive of Svidrigaylov's notion of hell (*Crime and Punishment*), is transformed into a garden image—surely a vision of Paradise. And Sarah Ruth, that flinty taskmistress of a harsh and exacting God, is, we may assume, finally placated.

But suddenly that O'Connor irony, which is predictable only in its unpredictableness, has both Parker and the reader spinning. Contrary to Parker's expectations, when Sarah Ruth sees the tattooed Christ, she at first recognizes nothing but "some more trash" of the sort she has regularly denounced. To Parker's question as to whether she doesn't really know who it is, she replies, "No. . . ." "It ain't anybody I know" (*ibid.*). At last, with a desperate cry, Parker announces, "It's him" . . . "God!" Enraged by what she considers the crowning blasphemy, Sarah Ruth snatches up a broom and, screaming, "Idolatry," begins to beat Parker mercilessly. As "large welts" form "on the face of the tattooed Christ," Parker stumbles into the yard and leans against a tree, crying. The author at this point enters the consciousness of Sarah Ruth to underscore the humor and pathos of this concluding scene:

> She stamped the broom two or three times on the floor and went to the window and shook it out to get the taint of him off it. Still gripping it, she looked toward the pecan tree and her eyes hardened still more. There he was—who called himself Obadiah Elihue—leaning against the tree, crying like a baby. (244)

The conclusion of the story is, to my taste, immensely satisfying and precisely because of a complexity and ambiguity not always found in Flannery O'Connor's fiction. The complexity derives in large measure, I feel, from an uncertainty as to where the author's sympathies lie. Admittedly, there is little doubt that the effect of the action of the story is to enlist our sympathies for Parker: anyone saddled with a narrow-minded, moralistic, shrewish wife such as Sarah Ruth is surely deserving of pity. (The stress in the final paragraph upon the hardness of Sarah Ruth's eyes tends to reinforce this impression.) Moreover, it is Parker who appears to be the more genuinely religious of the two; and, though in ignorance he has an image of God engraved on his body, it is he who has the experience of God as Spirit, not Sarah Ruth. She merely repeats, in somewhat mechanical fashion, familiar Biblical rhetoric: "He's a spirit. No man shall see his face" (*ibid.*). Finally, Parker's frustrated efforts to establish some form of communion with Sarah Ruth, his defenselessness against her withering, humiliating attack, and the despair he suffers as his dream of pleasing her collapses—all of these assuredly provide ample scope for our sympathy.

Then, too, in the "unfeeling voice" of Sarah Ruth are we not inclined to hear the voice of the stern, vengeful God of Southern fundamentalism, so ready to condemn, so reluctant to forgive? Most likely we are, but it would be a mistake therefore to dismiss Sarah Ruth as simply a religious fanatic embodying the least attractive aspects of Christianity and serving only as a foil to Parker. She is, indeed, deficient in that compassion and understanding that Louis Rubin4 finds so lacking in old Mason Tarwater of *The Violent Bear It Away*; as a person she has very little to offer in exchange for our sympathy. Yet it is she who brings Parker to his moment of self-recognition, to acceptance of the vocation implicit in his names, and to his experience of the cleansing power of God's judgment and mercy. We must remember, also, that it is her "icepick" eyes that prepare Parker for the knowledge that the "all-demanding" eyes of the Byzantine Christ reflect a Power that must be obeyed.

In other words, Sarah Ruth's role in the story is ambiguous and hence the difficulty we experience in attempting to "place" her in the value scheme that the story appears to present. In one sense she is an agent of God and plays a major part in bringing Parker to "salvation." Yet just as clearly she undermines that salvation with her utter and irrevocable rejection of him, leaving the reader with the slightly uncomfortable sensation of having observed a tragicomic figure tread his way through a Kafkaesque maze only to discover at the end a Power that is "all-demanding" but which he can never appease. Perhaps, in fact, this is exactly what Miss O'Connor intended. Presumably she takes Parker and his religious experience seriously. Yet her sense of humor and of proportion will not allow her to make him into a simple, unqualified twentieth-century prophet. Furthermore, it may have been her purpose to intimate, through the "mystifying" experience of Parker, the profound ambiguity of the numinous itself, its irreducibility to mere awefulness or mere wrath or mere graciousness. The God whom Parker encounters "speaks in one way, and in two"; and ostensibly he speaks through the "icepick" eyes of Sarah Ruth, as well as through the burning tree and shoes.

As "Parker's Back" ends, with that delightfully comic vignette of Sarah Ruth shaking the broom out the window to get the taint of Parker off it, while he stands against a pecan tree, weeping, there is nothing to suggest that the place of the secular and the natural has been usurped by the metaphysical and supernatural. The story ends, as it begins, with man in his natural setting, *i.e.*, with man in the society of his fellow men, seeking to know his identity and suffering the age-old pang of frustration as his search brings him into head-on collision with mysterious powers that he can neither ignore nor understand. And through these powers the metaphysical dimension of reality has made itself felt and felt decisively. The trick is to maintain the integrity of both the natural and the metaphysical. By refraining from writing an uplifting parable about the fall and redemption of a sinner, by consistently maintaining the comic tone, and by scrupulously guarding the naturalistic surface of the story so that it is not undermined by propagandistic motives, Flannery O'Connor has written a tale in which the true secular and the true sacred interpenetrate and sustain one another. In a way, Cheney is right: it *is* Flannery

O'Connor's characteristic method to travel from the natural to the metaphysical, but it is also characteristic of her method to carry the natural and secular along on the trip—not as "extras" for the amusement of the passengers but as essential cargo without which the voyage would be a dubious flight into empty spaces rather than a serious journey into the moral and spiritual center of humankind.

Notes

1. Brainard Cheney, "Miss O'Connor Creates Unusual Humor Out of Ordinary Sin," *Sewanee Review* 61 (Autumn 1963) 650.

2. Flannery O'Connor, "Parker's Back," *Everything That Rises Must Converge* (New York, 1965) 223. Subsequent page references will be found in parentheses in the text.

3. For several of the insights contained in this paragraph I am indebted to my friend Professor Giles B. Gunn of the University of Chicago at the time of my writing this article.

4. Louis D. Rubin, Jr., "Flannery O'Connor and the Bible Belt," *The Added Dimension: The Art and Mind of Flannery O'Connor,* Melvin J. Friedman and Lewis A. Lawson, eds. (New York, 1966) 63–64.

CPSIA information can be obtained
at www.ICGtesting.com
Printed in the USA
BVHW051659240323
661107BV00013B/502